*MW*

*4·14·*

# DATE DUE FOR RETURN

**)ES**

**f**

**)**
**s**

## Renewals
## www.liverpool.gov.uk/libraries
## 0151 233 3000

Edited by Ann Clayton

Researched by
Sid Lindsay
Bill Sergeant

2007

1

First published in Great Britain in 2007 by the

NOEL CHAVASSE VC MEMORIAL ASSOCIATION
Registered Charity No. 1112413


Copyright NCVCMA 2007

ISBN 978-0-9553495-1-5


All proceeds from the sale of this book will go towards the funding of a
Victoria Cross Memorial Statue in the City of Liverpool


Further copies, price £7.00 + p&p may be obtained from:

DONALD ALLERSTON
12 WEXFORD AVENUE
HALE VILLAGE
MERSEYSIDE L24 5RY
UNITED KINGDOM


Printed by Printstat, St. Helens, Merseyside, WA10 2PF, United Kingdom

# ontents

Foreword      5

| | | |
|---|---|---|
| 1. | Edward Felix BAXTER, VC | 7 |
| 2. | Eric Norman Frankland BELL, VC | 11 |
| 3. | Charles Henry COWLEY, VC | 15 |
| 4. | Eric Stuart DOUGALL, VC, MC | 19 |
| 5. | William DOWLING, VC | 23 |
| 6. | Arthur EVANS (Walter SIMPSON), VC, DCM | 27 |
| 7. | Donald Dickson FARMER, VC | 33 |
| 8. | (John) Vincent HOLLAND, VC | 41 |
| 9. | Alexander Malins LAFONE, VC | 47 |
| 10. | Frank LESTER, VC | 51 |
| 11. | Richard George MASTERS, VC | 55 |
| 12. | Patrick MYLOTT, VC | 59 |
| 13. | Thomas Patrick NEELY, VC, MM | 61 |
| 14. | George Edward NURSE, VC | 65 |
| 15. | Arthur Herbert PROCTER, VC | 71 |
| 16. | Joseph PROSSER, VC | 77 |
| 17. | Arthur Herbert Lindsay RICHARDSON, VC | 81 |
| 18. | John Alexander SINTON, VC | 91 |

Amendments to *Liverpool Heroes* Book 1      97

Appendix I : The Memorial      99

Appendix II : Sid Lindsay's Introduction to Book 1      101

Appendix III : NCVCMA pilgrimage to Belgium      107

# $\mathscr{F}$oreword
*by*
**Bill Sergeant**

While many readers will be familiar with our first book on 'Liverpool Heroes', no doubt some are taking the plunge for the first time, so I hope I will be forgiven for repeating myself to some extent!

I am chairman of the Noel Chavasse VC Memorial Association (NCVCMA), a charity established to commission, fund and erect a memorial statue in Liverpool to the memory of Chavasse VC & Bar, MC and fifteen other recipients of the Victoria Cross who were born here in the City. The stories of these sixteen brave men are told in *Liverpool Heroes - Book 1*, copies of which are still available. In the first book I outlined the origins and objectives of NCVCMA, and the sculptor commissioned to produce the memorial, Tom Murphy, explained the thought processes behind his design (reprinted in this book as **Appendix I**).

What I would like to do at this point is to bring you up to date with the somewhat slow progress we are making towards achieving our goal. The Memorial, which will be in bronze and will depict Chavasse, a Liverpool Scottish stretcher-bearer and a wounded soldier, will cost in the region of £105,000. To date, with the help of Windsor Developments (Liverpool) Limited and sizeable donations from members and friends of the Chavasse family and the RAMC, we have raised almost half of that amount. Tom Murphy has produced not only a small-scale model but also a full sized version from which a mould has been taken. The next step would be to authorise the foundry to start work on the finished article but before we do this we need to raise another £20,000. Raising a sum of that size is a difficult and slow process but we are confident that we will achieve it before too long. Once the memorial is produced, plaques will be affixed around the base to commemorate all sixteen heroes. In many cases this will be the only public acknowledgement of their deeds, and in some cases it will come almost 150 years after they earned their awards.

As part of our fundraising drive, we are producing a series of books, of which this is the second, which will recount the deeds and give some background to the lives of almost 60 Victoria Cross winners who are closely associated with Liverpool and its surrounding areas. All of the proceeds from sales of the books will go directly to our memorial fund. As I have already said, Book 1 dealt with those who were born in Liverpool as it existed at the time of their birth. (Chavasse was in fact born in Oxford but is undoubtedly an adopted son of Liverpool!) This second volume deals with the lives and exploits of another eighteen VC winners who lived within the city even though they were born in its outer suburbs or further afield. Book 3 will deal with others born close to the city, in areas like Seaforth, Crosby, and parts of Wirral, and Book 4 will take us slightly further to Widnes, St Helens, and Southport, and may also include others who served with the King's (Liverpool) Regiment.

I invite you to read the story so far in Books 1 and 2, and hope that your appetites will be whetted not only to read more but also to support our efforts to provide proper and long overdue recognition of Liverpool and Merseyside's heroes.

I will now repeat myself to this extent - most of the groundwork for this series of books was diligently and painstakingly done by a local historian, Sid Lindsay, who unfortunately passed away in 2006. I know that if Sid were still here he would be delighted and proud that his hard work had finally been published. He was instrumental in ensuring that unmarked graves of some of our heroes were given the sort of headstone and recognition they deserved, and I am confident that he would have been a keen supporter of our memorial project. To acknowledge our debt to Sid, we have incorporated into this book the introduction with which he prefaced his research file and which we used in Book 1 (**Appendix II** at the end of this book).

Interestingly, at a time when we are struggling to provide in Liverpool a fitting memorial to our many holders of the Victoria Cross, the Council at Tunbridge Wells has done just that for its heroes. In 2006, to celebrate the 400th birthday of Royal Tunbridge Wells, and also the 150th anniversary of the inception of the Victoria Cross, they commissioned the Poet Laureate, Andrew Motion, to write commemorative poetry, and Charles Gurney to design a memorial bearing the names of ten Victoria Cross holders, including Eric Dougall (featured in this book). The memorial depicts scenes from Motion's poem and is sited in 'Victoria Cross Grove', Dunorbin Park. Perhaps our City Council might take note!

Please read and enjoy these stories, in the knowledge that in doing so you are helping us to remember and commemorate, on behalf of the citizens of Liverpool, these very brave men of whom all of us can rightly be proud.

# ℰdward Felix Baxter VC

B orn on 18 September 1885 at Thornleigh, Hagley Road, Stourbridge, Worcestershire, Edward Baxter was the second son of Charles Albert Baxter, who had been a maltster, miller and corn merchant in Lower High Street, Stourbridge. The family was still living at Thornleigh in the 1891 Census but at about this time they moved to Mostyn, Shrubbery Street, Kidderminster. [Thornleigh is now a YMCA centre.] His mother, Beatrice, was the daughter of a local sporting personality Harry Sparrow. By 1901, the family had again moved, this time to Ivy Cottage, Hartlebury, Worcestershire, and Harold was boarding at Christ's Hospital, Christchurch, Newgate Street, London.

**Lieutenant Edward Felix Baxter VC**

He initially attended Hartlebury Grammar School and subsequently Christ's Hospital, London. He then took up employment with the United Counties Bank as a clerk, but in his early twenties left to become a tutor at Skerry's College, Rodney Street, Liverpool. This was a specialist establishment preparing young people for the civil service, the professions and commerce. It provided day and evening classes as well as postal courses, and was one of the foremost commercial schools of its type.

In 1906 Baxter married Leonora Mary Cornish, formerly of Kidderminster, in Liverpool and they lived at 5 Blantyre Road, Liverpool 15. Both he and his wife were keen competition motor cyclists, and were well known as such in the Midlands and North West. Edward won many prizes on the track and in hill climbing competitions. He raced many times at New Brighton and both he and

**5 Blantyre Road, L15. Marital home of Edward Felix Baxter VC**

his wife were members of the Liverpool Auto Cycle Club. Although Baxter competed in many motor cycling events, these were usually on the smaller circuits where the track was banked, but in 1910 he did compete in the Isle of Man Tourist Trophy Race. At that time the circuit in use was triangular in shape, starting and finishing at St. John's village green; it was 16 miles long, and had to be covered ten times. Baxter started well, but on the fourth lap narrowly failed to make the left hand corner at Ballacraine Hotel and hit the farmyard wall a hefty smack, bending the front forks of his cycle rather badly. He was not hurt and he tried desperately to lever the forks straight again, continuing in the race for a further lap. However, the machine would no longer steer properly, so he was forced to retire.

He and his wife both rode motor cycles built by the Rex Motor Manufacturing Company Limited, of Earlsdon, Coventry. His sister was also a great enthusiast. 'Baxter on a Rex' was a common reference to this gallant man wherever he went to compete - and he showed the same commitment to being a winner in a race as he did to leading his men.

[The Rex Company began as motor car manufacturers in Birmingham in 1899, and moved to Coventry the following year. That year at the National Show they demonstrated a 1.75 hp. motor cycle. Two brothers, Billy and Harold Williamson, were largely responsible for its early success, and were well acquainted and pleased with the reputation gained on the circuits by 'Baxter on a Rex', his wife and sister. George H. Hemingway took over from the Williamsons and there followed many engine and frame variations combining Rex with J.A.P. and Acme. In 1925 Wal Handley on a Rex-Acme became the first man to win two TT races in one week. The Rex Company closed down in 1930.]

At the outbreak of war in 1914, Baxter was at Skerry's College and became a motor cycle dispatch rider with the Mersey Defence Corps attached to the HQ staff in Rodney Street, Liverpool. He enlisted in September 1914 and soon gained promotion to sergeant. In September 1915 he was awarded a commission in the 1/8th (Irish) The King's (Liverpool) Regiment, and crossed to France with his battalion in January 1916, having trained as a bombing officer, a role which was unfortunately to cost him his life.

In the early weeks of their arrival in France the Liverpool Irish took part in numerous raids and sorties against the German lines, and Edward Baxter soon built a reputation for himself and his raiding party. Nicknamed 'The Forty Thieves', they caused havoc among the enemy, and on one raid their bombing cost the Germans 60 lives.

In a raid at Ransart, near Blairville, France, on 18 April 1916, Baxter earned his Victoria Cross. Prior to the raid, he was engaged during two nights on wire-cutting close to the enemy trenches. His men were cutting the wire while he was standing close by keeping watch on the enemy with a bomb in his hand ready to throw in the event of being detected. One of his men, moving forward, tripped on some of the cut wire knocking 2/Lt Baxter off balance and he dropped the grenade. He instantly picked it up, unscrewed the plug and removed the detonator and smothered it in the soil. By doing so he prevented the alarm being given and saved the lives of his men. Once the wire cutting had been completed, he placed himself at the head of the raiding party and dashed into the enemy trench. Meeting a German sentry who raised his rifle to fire, the lieutenant took hold of the weapon and threw it to one side, shooting the sentry with his revolver. He led his men through a maze of dugouts, bombing and shooting with such effect that the trench was soon cleared. He then climbed out of the trench and assisted each of his men over the parapet waiting to ensure that the last man was safely clear. He was not seen again. Search parties went out immediately, but to no avail. For a time it was thought that he may have been taken prisoner and he was reported missing, but later, through the American Embassy in Berlin, he was reported killed. His award was for most conspicuous bravery and devotion to duty, and his Commanding Officer, Colonel Fagan, wrote to Mrs. Baxter: 'The raid was successful, due to a great extent to the gallantry and resource of your husband. The men say that his gallantry and coolness were marvellous, and I have lost one of my best officers'.

Edward Baxter's brother, Lt Kenneth C. Baxter, who was well known as a cricketer in the Birmingham League, was also serving in France. There was now no need for Edward's wife to remain in Liverpool and she and her young daughter returned to live near her family in Kidderminster where she later remarried.

Gerald Gliddon in his series of books on 'VCs of the First World War': *Cambrai 1917*, describes how Baxter's body was first buried by the Germans in Boiry-Ste-Rictude churchyard. The Germans had put Baxter's name, rank and date of death on his headstone and this was noted by a fellow soldier, Arthur Kidd, when he visited the shelled churchyard in 1917. In 1925, Baxter's body was exhumed and reburied 25 miles away in Fillèvres British Cemetery. His Victoria Cross was presented to his widow at Buckingham Palace on 29 November 1916 by King George V and is now on display at the Imperial War Museum.

**Formerly Skerry's College. Edward Felix Baxter VC worked here as a tutor up to 1914.**

# ℰric Norman Frankland Bell VC

**Captain Eric Norman Frankland Bell VC**

Born on 28 August 1895 at Alma Terrace, Enniskillen, Fermanagh, Northern Ireland, Eric Bell was the youngest of three sons and one daughter of Edward Henry Bell and Dora Algeo Bell (nee Crowder). At the time of Eric's birth, his father was serving as a lieutenant quartermaster with the 2nd Battalion the Royal Inniskilling Fusiliers, at Thayetmyo, in Burma. When the regiment came back to this country it appears that they were stationed in Warrington for a time and it was here that the Bell family were reunited. Eric began his education at the 'People's College', which despite its grand name was an elementary school in Arpley Street, Warrington. When the family left Warrington, they went to live at 114 Upper Huskisson Street, Toxteth, Liverpool, although the 1901 Census shows the family living at 10 Alder Street, Seaforth, Liverpool, consisting of : Edward H. Bell (father), Dora A. Bell (mother), Alan G.F. Bell (born 1889), Irene D.F. Bell (born 1890), Haldane F. Bell (born 1892), Eric N. F. Bell (born 1895) and William S. R. Crowder (born 1881) a visitor born in Ireland. The initial 'F' in each of the children's names presumably stands for 'Frankland' and Crowder is presumably Dora's brother. Edward is shown as having been born in Devonport but his wife and children all seem to have been born in Ireland.

On 18 August 1902 young Eric was admitted to St. Margaret's School, in Prince's Avenue, Toxteth. From there, he went to the Liverpool Institute. The family moved again, to 22 University Road, Bootle. After leaving school, Eric entered the School of Architecture at Liverpool University, where he served as office boy to the eminent Professor Sir Charles Reilly. As a boy he had shown exceptional ability in art; as a student his progress was rapid. He was a musician of considerable skill and a talented linguist, and he had the natural qualities to display his ability in a most unpretentious manner. Quiet and reserved, he nevertheless got on well with all who knew him and he was not above giving other students help in their training.

He joined the Royal Inniskilling Fusiliers as a second lieutenant on 22 September 1914, and was posted to the 6th Battalion. Shortly afterwards, he was transferred to help form a nucleus for the 8th Battalion. He applied to join the Ulster Division, and was posted to the 9th Battalion of which his father was Adjutant. His two brothers, Alan George Frankland Bell and Haldane Frankland Bell, came respectively from America and Australia to join the regiment and were commissioned, a rare and admirable family affair. The Ulster Division moved to Seaford, on the Sussex coast and there Eric took advantage of several officers' courses and was again able to show his ability, this time as a soldier. In October 1915, the Division went to France. By now he was a lieutenant, trained in the new art of the trench mortar, and was in charge of a battery attached to the 9th Bn of the Inniskillings.

At Thiepval, on 1 July 1916, at the opening of the Battle of the Somme, Temp/Captain Eric N.F. Bell gave his life, but deservedly earned the Victoria Cross 'For most conspicuous bravery'. Eric was one of nine men awarded the Victoria Cross for their actions on this day. He was in command of 109 Trench Mortar Battery, and advanced from Thiepval Wood with the infantry in an attack upon the Schwaben Redoubt, a warren of tunnels and heavily fortified gun emplacements forming the axis of the German line. When the British front line was held up by enfilading machine-gun fire, Captain Bell crept forward and shot the machine-gunner. Later, on no less than three occasions, when British bombing parties which were clearing the enemy's trenches were unable to advance, he went forward alone and threw trench-mortar bombs among the enemy. When he had no more bombs available, he stood on the parapet, under intense fire, and used a rifle with great coolness and effect on the enemy advancing to counter-attack. Finally, he was killed while rallying and reorganising groups of infantry who had lost their officers. All this was outside the scope of his normal duties with his battery, and as a result he sacrificed his life. He had not yet reached his 21st birthday.

Professor Sir Charles Reilly, was always most economical with praise of other men, yet he wrote: 'Eric was one of the few men I know who could have won such an honour (the Victoria Cross) without being spoilt by it. He was as modest as he proved to be brave. He had the sensitive temperament of the real artist'.

Many years later Charles Reilly wrote in his autobiography, somewhat pompously:

> *One day my office boy Bell appeared in uniform. The next time he came he was back from France and a very different person from the shy, timid youth I had known. He was to have a commission in the Inniskillings in which his father had held one. He was possessed I remember with the need for everyone to join up or do something. The boy who had run like a hare whenever I had shouted for him, told me, when I cross-examined him, how he had been out between the lines at night. He was to go back - lead an attack, be killed and given the V.C. posthumously. Dear little, timid Bell, who loved me like a child - a V.C. and dead.*

The Professor had not forgotten him.

Sir Edward Carson, famous barrister and politician wrote: 'He died a noble death'. Sir Alfred Dale, Vice-Chancellor of Liverpool University, paid this tribute to Eric Bell's parents: 'Your pride must be as great as your sorrow, and we, in our measure share in both, but even now you must be thankful that you had so much to give, and gave it'. Such were the many letters of praise for this young man, and of sympathy for his parents. His nature belied the true strength of character that enabled him to display such outstanding courage; he was a man far beyond his tender years. If he had survived, there is no telling how far his talents may have taken him.

His father received a letter from King George V which read: 'It is a matter of sincere regret to me that the death of Captain E.N.F. Bell, deprived me of the pride of personally conferring on him the Victoria Cross, the greatest of all rewards for bravery and devotion to duty'.

Eric Bell died near Thiepval, one of the 5,500 casualties of the 36th Ulster Division on that first day of the Battle of the Somme. His body was never recovered and he is remembered on the Thiepval Memorial. The nearby Ulster Division Memorial takes the form of a tower, a replica of the memorial to Helen, the mother of the Marquis of Dufferin, that stands at Clanboye, Co. Down, Northern Ireland, where the Division did so much of its training.

Eric Bell's father, Captain Edward H. Bell, was instrumental in forming several battalions for service overseas, and carried out a number of important duties at Gallipoli, Egypt and in the Libyan Desert, returning to serve in France. It seems that in the early 1920s Capt. and Mrs. Bell emigrated to live near one of the sons. Their daughter Irene went to live in Larne, Co. Antrim, in Northern Ireland. Both of Eric's brothers were seriously wounded in action and at the time of his death were hospitalised in this country. It is believed that they returned to their respective adopted homes in America and Australia.

Captain Eric Norman Frankland Bell VC was an exceptionally talented young man who gained much notice as an artist and as a person in the few years that he lived. The website of Liverpool Institute Old Boys (Liobians) records that in 1933 Eric Bell's VC was taken by his sister to New Zealand, where it remained for almost 70 years. She was the stepmother of Air Marshal Sir Richard Bolt KBE CB DFC AFC, Royal New Zealand Air Force, who was New Zealand's Chief of Defence Staff between 1976 and 1980. She gave him Eric's Victoria Cross shortly before she died. In 2001, Sir Richard arranged for its return to the Inniskillings' Regimental Museum in Enniskillen Castle. Having been displayed in the Regimental Depot Mess on a Dinner Night in February 2001, it was handed over to the Regiment by Colonel Stewart Douglas OBE, the Colonel of the Royal Irish Regiment, on 15 February 2001.

# *C*harles Henry Cowley VC

It is believed that Charles Henry Cowley was born on 21 February 1872, in Baghdad, Iraq, the son of Commander Henry V. Cowley, of the Eastern Telegraph Service. He is said to have been educated in Liverpool at Mr. Strut's School, although it has been impossible to establish the whereabouts of this establishment. However, in the 1881 Census there is a list of boarding pupils at the 'Frodsham Academy' in Main Street, Frodsham, in which appears the name of Charles Cowley, born in Baghdad, Asia, aged 8 years. It seems highly likely that this is Charles Cowley VC.

**Charles Henry Cowley VC**

Charles Cowley joined the training ship HMS *Worcester* in January 1885, serving for over three years before leaving in 1888 with a first class extra certificate and an ordinary certificate. HMS *Worcester* was a 1500-ton two-deck ship of the line which was given by the Government as the base for a maritime training school founded in 1862 to provide properly trained officers for the Merchant Marine. It has been described as London's answer to HMS *Conway* which at the time was moored on the Mersey. There was great sporting rivalry between the two and on 11 June 1891 the two ships took part in the first of what was to become an annual event by racing against each other on the Mersey. (For the record, *Conway* won by 12 lengths!). In 1888, Cowley joined the firm of McDrummond & Co. and sailed in the vessel *Pendragon*.

To return to the Liverpool connection, the 1891 Census shows him living with his aunt, Jane Netherton, a widow born in Cork, together with two other boys, described as her nephews and named George V.Cowley aged 12 and Robert G.Cowley aged 6 years. Charles Henry Cowley is described as a 'sailor' born in Baghdad in about 1872. George and Robert, his younger brothers, are also said to have been born in Baghdad. The family, at that time, was living at 3 Monastery Road, Liverpool, the boys being in the care of their aunt while their parents were abroad. Jane Netherton seems to have been the sister of Captain Cowley as in 1881 she is shown living at 6 Monastery Road with her four children and her mother, Jane Chartres Cowley. In 1901, at 19 Windsor Road, Liverpool, Jane was living with her own daughter and a niece, Millicent D.Cowley, born in Baghdad in 1888.

After some time at sea Charles H. Cowley returned to his family in Baghdad, and took up employment with the Lynch Company, founded in 1839 by Lt H.B. Lynch, a former British officer with the Indian Navy. Lynch operated a regular service between Baghdad and Basra with four iron steamers traversing the River Tigris. He had a degree of monopoly with the service although the Pasha of Baghdad had introduced some competition. Cowley was very familiar with the local scenario, had many Arab friends and was fluent in the language. He was also well versed in the river lore and vagaries of the currents. He became a first class river pilot, and in the course of his journeys gathered information as an intelligence agent which was extremely useful to the British authorities in the early months of the Great War.

When war broke out in 1914, he was in command of the river steamer *Mejideh*, and continued his regular runs until war with Turkey became imminent; as an RNVR Lieutenant Commander he knew where his duty clearly lay. The assembly of the River Flotilla for the assault on the Shatt-el-Arab delta and the defence of Basra required an assortment of shallow draft vessels but, more importantly, they needed the invaluable experience of Charles Cowley.

In September 1915, the British and Indian forces advancing on Baghdad captured the fortress town of Kut-el-Amara only to find that they could make no further progress. They became besieged in this 'God-forsaken spot in this pest and disease ridden country'. All attempts to relieve the garrison were frustrated and from December 1915 to April 1916 the plight of the trapped forces was wretched in the extreme. Desperate measures were called for to try to get supplies through rather than surrender the town and allow the residents to suffer at the hands of the Turks. The steamer *Julnar* was chosen for the run and was prepared with additional plating and sandbagging to offer some protection from gunfire. She was loaded with 270 tons of supplies and her crew of three officers and eleven men were all unmarried volunteers. Lt H.O.B. Firman RN was in command, Charles H. Cowley, was second in command, and Sub-Lt W.L. Reed RNR was the engineering officer.

It had been hoped that creating distractions about the operation and departure of the relief ship would enable her to make good progress up river before encountering enemy gunfire, but as is so often the case total secrecy was almost impossible. On 24 April the *Julnar* left Falihiyah at 8 pm, a dark, moonless night, and soon found herself the target of unremitting machine gun fire. They pressed on, knowing the desperate urgency of their mission but were shelled by heavy artillery at Magasis. Here the Turks had stretched steel hawsers across the river and set their artillery on target, so that as the *Julnar* arrived at this point towards midnight she was met with a terrific barrage at almost point-blank range. Her bridge was smashed and Lt Firman was killed along with members of the crew. The wire hawsers became entangled round the ship's rudder; she was now out of control and ran aground. As she did so, the Turks rushed on board, capturing the remaining crew and the vital supplies for Kut. The 'do or die' attempt to relieve the besieged garrison had failed, but no one could deny the extraordinary courage and application of the men of the *Julnar*, who had continued their illfated journey against the odds.

The following day the garrison could see that their only hope of survival was lying amongst the reeds some miles away, and a few days later General Townshend was obliged to surrender his force of some 9,000 British and Indian troops into the hands of the Turks. Charles Cowley was alive but slightly wounded when he was taken prisoner on the ship, but was separated from the rest of his crew as they were led away. He was never seen again and later the Turks reported that he had been shot attempting to escape. He had always maintained that if ever he was taken by the Turks he would almost certainly be killed because his life in Mesopotamia made him an Ottoman subject in their eyes and they would regard him as a traitor.

Lieutenant Commander Charles Cowley RNVR was at the wheel for that fateful journey as he piloted the vessel through the hazards of the winding Tigris, and was exposed to the harrowing fire of the enemy throughout. He knew that death was likely to be the result of the mission, yet he remained at his post regardless in the hope that the garrison would be saved. For their courage, both he and Lt H.B. Firman were awarded the Victoria Cross.

Cowley's mother received his Victoria Cross from Rear Admiral Wade, the senior naval officer, Persian Gulf, on the afternoon of 25 August 1917. His name appears on the Basra Memorial, Iraq, together with the names of Lt Firman and members of the crew he commanded.

[Note: in an earlier attempt to relieve Kut-el-Amara in January 1916, John Sinton (see p.97) earned his Victoria Cross.]

# Eric Stuart Dougall
## VC MC

Eric Stuart Dougall was born on 13 April 1886 at 'Brookside', Auckland Road, Tunbridge Wells, the only son of Andrew and Emily E. Dougall. Andrew Dougall was the engineer and general manager of the Tunbridge Wells Gas Company. Eric was educated at Tonbridge School, where he won an exhibition in 1904 to Pembroke College, Cambridge to read Natural Sciences. He graduated with a third class degree in the Mechanical Sciences Tripos in 1908. He represented Cambridge at inter-university sports in 1906, 1907 and in 1908, in the half mile and mile events, and ran a cross country race in 1906 against Oxford. [It is likely that he ran against N.G.Chavasse, VC & Bar, in these events.]

Lieut. (Acting Captain) E.S. Dougall

On leaving Cambridge, he became an engineer with the Mersey Docks and Harbour Board in Liverpool, under A.G. Lyster, where he remained until 1912. Dougall was a member of both the Liverpool Pembroke Athletics Club and Liverpool R.U. Football Club when he was living at 17, Kimberley Street, Toxteth, Liverpool 8, presumably in lodgings. He was then appointed Assistant Engineer to the Bombay Port Trust. Here he became a popular figure and joined the Bombay Light Horse. In early 1916 he obtained leave of absence to come back to England to apply for a commission in the Army, and was accepted in the Royal Field Artillery. Almost at once he was on his way to France and the battlefields.

His diaries show that he was in the fighting zone most of the time. In July 1917 he was awarded the Military Cross for conspicuous gallantry and devotion to duty when, as a Group Intelligence Officer and Forward Observation Officer, he took up a succession of observation posts in advanced and exposed positions from which he successfully maintained communications with headquarters. He was slightly wounded but remained on duty, and frequently performed work requiring initiative under heavy fire with great coolness and gallantry. This was during the battle of Messines, the preliminary battle before the advance on Passchendaele. He was also gazetted Acting Captain.

During March and April 1918 he was continuously in action during the early stages of the German offensive, and was promoted to the rank of major in the latter month. At Messines again he earned his Victoria Cross, listed on the Special Reserve, attached 'A' Battery, 88th Brigade, RFA. The citation from the *London Gazette* of 31 May 1918 reads as follows:

*For most conspicuous bravery and skilful leadership in the field when in command of his battery. Captain Dougall maintained his guns in action from early morning throughout a heavy concentration of gas and high explosive shell. Finding he could not clear the crest, owing to the falling back of our line, Captain Dougall ran his guns on to the top of the ridge to fire over open sights. By this time our infantry had been pressed back in line with the guns. Captain Dougall at once assumed command of the situation, rallied and organized the infantry, supplied them with Lewis guns, and armed as many gunners as he could spare with rifles. With these he formed a line in front of his battery, which during this period was harassing the advancing enemy with a rapid rate of fire. Although exposed to both rifle and machine gun fire, this officer fearlessly walked about as though on parade, calmly giving orders and encouraging everybody. He inspired the infantry with his assurance that 'so long as you stick to your trenches I will keep my guns here'. This line was maintained right through the day, thereby delaying the enemy's advance for over 12 hours. In the evening, having expended all ammunition, the battery received the order to withdraw. This was done by man-handling the guns over a distance of about 800 yards of shell cratered country, an almost impossible feat considering the ground and intense machine gun fire. Owing to Captain Dougall's personality and skilful leadership throughout this trying day, there is no doubt that a serious breach in our line was averted.*

Dougall was killed four days later while directing his battery's fire. The Adjutant wrote at this time: 'a finer man never breathed, and his place in the brigade can never be filled'. He was killed in the attack on Mount Kemmel, on 14 April 1918, one day after his 32nd birthday. His grave is in the Westoutre British Cemetery, 11km south west of Ypres. The cemetery register lists him as 'Major' Dougall.

His father by this time had been forced, through ill-health, to resign from the Gas Company, and it appears that his mother also was seriously indisposed, for his sister, Miss E.M. Dougall, went to Buckingham Palace, to receive both his Military Cross and his Victoria Cross from the King at a private investiture.

In 1969, his sister bequeathed to Pembroke College a number of Eric S. Dougall's medals, including his Victoria Cross and Military Cross, together with a series of related documents: his brief diaries for the years 1917 and 1918, and a letter to his father from King George V concerning the award of the VC. These, together with a photograph of the gallant man and some other items, are kept in the Pembroke Library. The Cambridge Alumni Magazine in 2006 quoted from Dougall's diary the passage containing his account of the events which led to his award: 'Hun attacked. Fought guns all day until 7pm and then got them all out to

**Eric Stuart Dougall's headstone at Westoutre in Belgium**

behind Wytschaete. Moved on to Klein Vierstraat'. The account is brief and deliberately understates his deeds – a modesty shared by many of our 'Liverpool Heroes'.

On 7 December 1986, Liverpool Cricket Club, established in Aigburth, Liverpool since 1881, opened two refurbished lounges, and named them the Chavasse Room (after N.G.Chavasse VC & Bar), and the Dougall Room. Each room contains a portrait and copy of the respective citations. The official opening of these rooms was performed by the Lord Lieutenant of Merseyside. It is a very laudable tribute paid by the club to two gallant men who were only members for a short while some 80 years ago.

# *W*illiam Dowling VC

William Dowling is believed to have been born in 1825, at Thomastown in Co. Kilkenny, Ireland. He joined the 32nd Regiment of Foot (later to become the Duke of Cornwall's Light Infantry) in 1845, and for most of his service he was abroad, mainly in Eastern India.

Although Private Dowling did not take kindly to Army life, he was at least being fed and clothed and for most of the time was provided with accommodation. Life in Ireland must have been desperately hard for men like him and no doubt his up-bringing made him a survivor. From this standpoint the Army took care of what he regarded as the essentials and would manage the rest of his life. He turned out to be one of the worst characters in his regiment and his reputation was so bad that it is one of the few things that anybody can learn about him 150 years later.

During the Indian Mutiny at Lucknow in 1857, this troublesome soldier established himself as a hero of the regiment. Lucknow, as the headquarters of Sir Henry Lawrence and his administration in the Oudh province, had experienced mutinies but the garrison had not been attacked. On 30 June, Lawrence intended moving out to clear some of the pockets of rebels in the outlying districts, and soon found himself in such difficulty that he and his depleted force had to withdraw back into the enclave known as The Residence. This was a group of buildings with connecting perimeter walls which formed what might be loosely described as a fort. The garrison, which consisted of some 1,720 soldiers, including 712 loyal Sepoys and 153 civilian volunteers, found itself beleaguered. Lawrence was mortally wounded by a rebel shell on 4 July, and the command fell to Brigadier General John Inglis. There were more than 200 women and 230 children in the enclave during the siege, and all were aware of the atrocities that had been perpetrated in other areas by the mutineers.

The gallantry which earned Dowling the Victoria Cross was demonstrated on three occasions over a period of three months, and it can be said that his behaviour throughout the siege was in complete contrast to that which earned him his dreadful reputation. His citation in the *London Gazette* on 21 November 1859 read as follows:

> *For distinguished gallantry on the 4th July 1857, in going out with two other men, since dead, and spiking two of the enemy guns. He killed a Subadar of the enemy who was by one of the guns.*

> *For distinguished gallantry on the 9th of the same month, in going out again with three men, since dead, to spike one of the enemy guns. He had to retire, the spike being too small, but was exposed to the same risk.*

> *Also for distinguished bravery, on the 27th September 1857, in spiking an 18 pounder gun during a sortie, he being at the same time under a most heavy fire from the enemy.*

In the siege of Lucknow from 30 June to 25 September 1857, the 32nd Regiment was the only British unit holding the garrison against a vastly superior rebel force some 20,000 strong. William Dowling had been promoted to corporal during this time, and he took his responsibility seriously, being mentioned, with others, in a dispatch from the Chief Engineer of the Oudh Field Force. In the siege, the holding force had to mine and countermine, to prevent the enemy from completing his underground tunnels and placing explosives under strategic objectives. It was a difficult and extremely dangerous operation, requiring a great deal of physical stamina and courage. Many of the men recruited from Cornwall had gained experience working in the Cornish tin mines, and it was reported afterwards that the garrison had constructed at least 21 shafts, totalling more than 200 feet in depth, and had cut nearly 4000 feet of galleries adjoining the shafts. Many times the galleries of both sides were so close to each other that it was possible to listen to movements and even converse, as happened when some rebels attempted to persuade a number of loyal sepoys away from their digging to join them. Captain Crommelin, the Chief Engineer, in his dispatch to the Governor General dealing with 'The Final Engineering Offensive Operations' concluded:

> *I cannot close this report, without noticing, in the most favourable manner, the important services performed by the undermentioned soldiers, as superintendents of the miners - A/Sergeants Cullimore, Banetta, and Farrer; and Corporal Dowling, all of the 32nd*

*Regiment; with Corporal Hosey, of the Madras Fusiliers; Private Baylan, of the 5th Fusiliers. Their duties have been of a very dangerous and arduous character, and have invariably been performed to my complete satisfaction.*

On 25 September a relief column under General Sir Henry Havelock, after a most remarkable forced march, broke through the investing rebel lines and linked up with the garrison of Lucknow, but the siege was only lifted 53 days later, by General Sir Colin Campbell with the full weight of the main British force. The casualties of the 32nd Regiment were 379 killed or died, and 209 wounded out of a total of about 700 (all ranks).

Dowling was eventually promoted to sergeant. This and the award of the VC are said to have been instrumental in reforming him from his previous bad ways. He attended the Investiture at Windsor Castle, on 4 January 1860, as one of the 24 recipients who were presented by HM Queen Victoria with their medals at a parade in the quadrangle. The garrison of Windsor, consisting of the 1st Regiment of Life Guards and the 2nd Battalion Grenadier Guards were in attendance. The Queen was accompanied by Prince Albert, together with the Prince of Wales, Princess Alice, Prince Arthur, Prince Leopold, and Princess Beatrice. Also in attendance were the Duke of Cambridge, as GOC, the Rt. Hon. Sir Sidney Herbert, Secretary of State for War, and many other dignitaries. It was a far cry from Dowling's early impoverished upbringing.

William Dowling was married and in the 1881 Census was listed as living at 2, Rokeby Street, Everton, Liverpool, with his wife Maria, who was born in 1836 in Ireland, and their two children, Joseph F. born in 1864 in Ireland, a commercial clerk, and Maria, born in Ireland in 1866. William is described as being a customs officer, an occupation which he took up upon his return to Liverpool after being pensioned from the Army. He died in Stanley Hospital on 17 February 1887, of bronchitis, aged 63 years. In 1901, Maria, his widow, was living at 33 Bartlett Street, Wavertree, Liverpool, with her son, Joseph, now an insurance agent, his wife Elsie, born in Shrewsbury, and their daughter, Wilhelmina, born in 1901 in Liverpool. Maria died in 1904.

William Dowling's burial place was for many years unknown but thanks to the efforts of Maurice Rigby it was eventually established that he had been buried in the Liverpool Roman Catholic Cemetery (Ford Cemetery). The exact location of his grave is still uncertain but on 16 January 1990 a service of dedication was held at the cemetery when a memorial plaque of carved Cornish slate was unveiled. The ceremony was attended by a 50-strong group, including the Mayor of Sefton Council, Joe Lynch GC BEM and Major W.H.White of the Duke of Cornwall's Light Infantry Regimental Museum. Buglers from the Queen's Light Infantry at Preston played the Last Post and Reveille, while an Irish piper played a lament. The service was conducted by the Kirkdale Parish Priest, Father Michael Reilly.

Unfortunately, less than two weeks before the service, Ford Cemetery was the subject of vandalism by local youths, resulting in £10000 worth of damage. In view of this, Laurence Furlong of the Catholic Cemeteries Board arranged with Father Reilly for the plaque to be reinstalled in the Parish Church.

Dowling's Victoria Cross is currently on display in the Duke of Cornwall's Light Infantry Museum at Bodmin, Cornwall. [Sid Lindsay discovered that it was once sold, on 31 October 1924, for £51.00.]

**Memorial plaque at Ford Cemetery**

WITHIN THIS CEMETERY LIES
SERJEANT WILLIAM DOWLING V.C.
32ND (CORNWALL) LIGHT INFANTRY
1825 – 1887
OF THOMASTOWN, CO. KILKENNY
AWARDED THE VICTORIA CROSS FOR HIS
GALLANTRY AT LUCKNOW ON 4TH AND
9TH JULY AND 27TH SEPTEMBER 1857

# ✐rthur Evans
# (Walter Simpson) VC

A rthur Evans was born on 8 April 1891 at 33 Caradoc Road, Seaforth, Litherland, near Liverpool, the son of Robert and Eleanor Ann Evans (nee McCann). Robert had married Eleanor early in 1879 and in 1881 they were living with Eleanor's widowed father Samuel, and his son James, at 16 Myrtle Street, Birkenhead. They already had two daughters, Eleanor and Sarah. Robert at this time is said to have been a storekeeper at an engineering works. In 1901, Robert and Eleanor were living at 33 Caradoc Road, with four other children including Arthur, and Robert is described as a 'Timekeeper (Mercantile)'. Arthur was educated at St. Thomas's School, Seaforth.

From this point his story is one of mystery, and it is unlikely that the complete truth will ever be known. There are a number of reports from what appear to be reliable sources although some of the details are in conflict. The first of these concerns his name: he was awarded the Victoria Cross under the name of Walter Simpson.

A lengthy report in the *Bolton Journal & Guardian*, dated 1 November 1918, stated:

> *Sergeant Simpson is just the man to have won the V.C. for his life has been one of romantic adventure since boyhood. His official home is at 99, Davenport Street (Bolton), the residence of his stepsister, Miss Evans, but his family really hails from Liverpool. He has spent all his leaves in Bolton. His stepbrother, Mr. J.R. Evans, who lives at 48, Church St. has also been in the Army, and another member of the family, Private James Evans is still out. With the exception of a few months this family has been represented at the Front right from the outbreak.*

> *The sergeant himself joined up three weeks before the war started. He was enamoured of the air service, and joined the ranks with a view to getting a transference. He was in the King's Liverpools, and before he could do anything found himself sailing with the first Expeditionary Force as probably the youngest member in point of length of service,*

*in the gallant 'Contemptibles'. He fought at Mons like an old hand, and held on with tenacity until Festubert, in May of 1915, when he was wounded. He went to hospital at Manchester, but was restless, and eventually asked for discharge from the 'blue cloth'. He was transferred to the Devons, went out to France with the Training Corps, was put in the North Staffs, then in a Territorial Battalion of the Lincolnshires, and eventually settled with a regular battalion from the same county.*

*In October 1917, Sergeant Simpson was gassed and wounded, and found himself in hospital at Bath. Again he asked for his discharge, came to Bolton for a brief spell, and then went to Ireland. As on the previous occasion he asked to be sent to the Front, and spent his last leave at home at Whitsuntide this year. He said to his sister then 'Nothing will do for me now except the V.C. I will bring home the V.C. and peace not in pieces'.*

*Starting in the ranks, he eventually became an N.C.O., a Sergeant, reverting to Corporal on going to the front this year, but he has now got three stripes again. He is a born soldier. He is only 27 years of age now, so that he was but 23 when he was Mentioned in the first Dispatches issued by Lord French. On one occasion since he went out Sergeant Simpson was unofficially reported killed. As a matter of fact, he had been buried, he and his beloved machine-gun, and when he recovered from the shock of a shell explosion he found only his face exposed to the air. He was speedily dug out by two comrades.*

*Of adventures at the Front he has had more than his share, for he is a brave soldier, but all his life he has loved romance, and he is the subject for a fascinating and thrilling story.*

*His father put him in an office when he was a boy. It was a case of a square peg and the round hole, and son Walter threw down the pen and took up the shovel – in the Navy. It was not long before he was out, however, invalided with smashed ribs. But he had tasted adventure, and he at once joined the merchant service. Be it whispered - somewhere across the Atlantic he deserted his ship, and the next time he was heard of he had charge of a thousand natives working on the construction of the Panama Canal. Even that was tame, and he was soon one of three whites - the others were an Australian and a Scotsman - who were taking an exploration party into the interior of South America. Three times he fell sick with fever, and was brought back to the coastal base by native women.*

*Then he became homesick, and the longing was so great that he determined to work his way back. He came back home in a very roundabout way, however. First he went to Cuba, next he was in Buffalo, Detroit, and later he saw the water tumbling over Niagara. He took any old job on his journey, and was once a waiter in a hotel. At New York he joined a sailing vessel, and worked his way via Australia to Liverpool, thus completing his journey round the world by taking a twelve months voyage. On board the vessel by a singular coincidence, he met the late Dr. Garstang's son, Robert, who also completed the 12 month's trip. Sergeant Simpson, by the way, is a good French linguist, and has a smattering of other tongues. He can converse with almost any man.*

Evans earned his Victoria Cross while serving with the 6th Battalion of the Lincolnshire Regiment (33rd Brigade, llth Division), at a place south-west of Etaing, France, on 2 September 1918. The citation was as follows:

*For most conspicuous bravery and initiative when with a daylight patrol sent out to reconnoitre and to gain touch with a neighbouring division. When on the west bank of a river an enemy machine-gun post was sighted on the east bank. The river being too deep to ford, Sgt. Simpson volunteered to swim across, and having done so, crept up alone in rear of the machine-gun post. He shot the sentry and also a second enemy who ran out; he then turned out and caused four more of the enemy to surrender. A crossing over the river was subsequently found, and the officer and one man of his patrol joined him, and reconnaissance was continued along the riverbank. After proceeding some distance, machine-gun and rifle fire was opened on the patrol and the officer was wounded. In spite of the fact that no cover was available, Sergeant Simpson succeeded in covering the withdrawal of the wounded officer under the most dangerous and difficult conditions, and under heavy fire. The success of the patrol, which cleared up a machine-gun post on the flank of the attacking troops of a neighbouring division and obtained an identification, was greatly due to the very gallant conduct of Sergeant Simpson.*

There can be no doubt at all about Arthur Evan's bravery, as he was awarded the Distinguished Conduct Medal a few weeks later. *The London Gazette* of 2 December 1919 carried the following report:

*Award of the Distinguished Conduct Medal. To 41788 Sergeant A. Evans, 6th Battalion Lincolnshire Regiment. For great courage and initiative near Cambrai. He was in charge of a platoon acting as a fighting patrol on the night of 6/7th October 1918, with instructions to clear the country north of the Chateau of Aubencheu-au-Bac to the Canal-de-la-Sensée. A strong enemy post was encountered. He promptly rushed the post killing ten, wounding several, and taking one prisoner. The prisoner secured afforded most valuable information. He has shown excellent leadership and the utmost disregard of all danger.*

Information from the Lincolnshire Regiment (The Royal Anglian Regiment), states that Arthur Evans enlisted in the King's Liverpool Regiment at the outbreak of war, deserted, and joined the Merchant Navy as 'Arthur Evans' (his real name). He served at sea for a year but the excitement was not enough for him and he again deserted, joining the Lincolnshire Regiment. Presumably he chose the county regiment because he had landed at Grimsby, although he had no other connections with the county. On making a break from his past service he decided to change his name. He chose Walter Simpson, possibly after the Colonel of the Regiment at the time, Major General C.R. Simpson. After the war, he reverted to his correct name of Arthur Evans. He was decorated with the Victoria Cross by King George V at Fresnes, in France, early in December 1918.

Recent information confirms that he did desert the King's Regiment, and this must have been in late 1915, for a Regimental report shows that he was entitled to hold the 1914-1915 Star. It also shows that he received the Mercantile Marine Medal. The London Gazette of 31 March 1919, stated:

*Notification of award of Victoria Cross to 41788 Corporal (Lance Sergeant) Walter Simpson, 6th Battalion, Lincolnshire Regiment, as announced in the London Gazette dated 3rd October 1918, should read as awarded to Corporal (Lance Sergeant) Arthur Evans, 6th Battalion, Lincolnshire Regiment, the latter being the correct Christian name and Surname of this N.C.O. which he has been permitted to re-assume.*

It is believed that after the war he went to America and then returned to England. In 1924 he married Miss H.M. Whittaker of Woodside, Wimbledon, London. They emigrated to New Zealand, where he obtained employment as an instructor in the Defence Department. In 1928, they moved to Sydney Australia, and he joined the Australian Tank Corps but was invalided out suffering from the after-effects of gassing during the First World War.

Sergeant Arthur Evans VC, DCM, died on 31 October 1936 after a long and painful illness. Major E.T. Penfold, Commanding Officer of the Tank Corps, wrote in the Australian Army magazine:

*Any person who was privileged to know Sergeant Arthur Evans could not help being struck by the personality and grit of this fine soldier. Although small in stature, he was particularly staunch of purpose - a good friend and a very loyal subject of His Majesty the King.*

*There were times when perhaps Australia did not treat him as well as it might, but such was his nature that he took his knocks with a grin and came up smiling and without losing heart.*

*One can never forget his immense joy when his wife presented him with a son, after I think twelve years of married life. For the last two or three years, the gas which had affected his stomach, began to play havoc with him and he was to spend increasing periods of time in the Prince of Wales Hospital.*

*Born in Liverpool, Sergeant Evans always carried the trace of the accent which is attributable to men of that district. He joined the Lincolnshire Regiment at the outbreak of the war and served with that regiment for some nine years, going after the war to India, where he served with the colours for five years.*

So there have been three versions of the life of Arthur Evans VC, DCM, all varying in the details, and strangely there is a slight similarity with the early life and travels of Joseph Tombs VC (who went to sea, served as a mercenary in a border dispute in Peru, worked on the construction of the Panama Canal and lived in the USA; Tombs' story will be featured in *Liverpool Heroes* Book 3). One wonders if they knew each other at all. Certainly Arthur Evans's life appears to have been a full one up to the time of his health failing and if he did desert the King's Regiment in 1915 and had been caught the story of his life would have ended just there.

He was given a military funeral in Sydney, and among the mourners were seven VC holders, as well as members of his last unit of the Australian Tank Corps who were given the honour of firing a final volley over the coffin. It is claimed that as the Tank Corps only had revolvers as their personal weapons their use on this occasion was the first time this had been done in Australia. After the funeral the seven VCs launched an appeal for a fund to support his widow and three-year-old son, who was also named Arthur.

Even in death, Arthur Evans continued to provide a touch of mystery that adds to his story. A year after his death George VI was to be crowned King in London; Evans' ashes were passed into the care of Arthur Percy Sullivan VC, a former Corporal of the 45th Battalion of the Royal Fusiliers. [Sullivan had won his medal in action near the Sheika River in North Russia on 10 August 1919.] Sullivan was a member of the Australian contingent attending the Coronation. He had been a close friend of Arthur Evans, and his first duty after arrival in the UK was to hand over the ashes to Arthur's relatives. The ashes were buried at Park Cemetery, Lytham St. Annes, Lancashire, on 29 March 1937.

On 9 April, Arthur Percy Sullivan collapsed and died outside Wellington Barracks, just eleven days after he had completed his solemn duty to his comrade. There is a plaque outside the Barracks, on Birdcage Walk, London, in memory of this gallant man's tragic death.

Arthur Evans is the only VC whose remains are interred at Park Cemetery, Lytham. His grave, No. A483 in the Church of England section, was purchased by Mrs. Annie Gertrude Evans to bury Mr. John Robert Evans, who died in March 1933, aged 49 years. The next interment was of Arthur Evans's ashes, and then Mrs. A. G. Evans was buried there on 15 February 1945. She was aged 58 years. J.R. Evans was referred to in the report of 1918, in the Bolton newspaper, as Arthur Evans's stepbrother, and it seems that Annie was his wife.

The *Liverpool Echo*, in reporting Evans' death in Australia in 1936, stated that his father and mother were still alive and living in Sandy Road, Seaforth. Checking the Liverpool Directory for that year, there is an entry for John Simpson, clerk, living at 23, Sandy Road. It is possible that his natural parents split up and his mother remarried giving him the opportunity to use both surnames, although the use of the name Simpson would not have had any legal standing, hence his reuse of Evans after the war. We must presume that Evans' wife and son remained in Australia, but it seems strange that such efforts were made to bring his remains back to this country and bury them in Lytham. The records show that his Victoria Cross is not publicly held.

**Evans family grave at Park Cemetery Lytham**

32

# *D*onald Dickson Farmer VC

**Donald Dickson Farmer VC**

D onald Farmer was born on 28 May 1877 at 5 Winchester Row, Kelso, Roxburghshire, Scotland. He was the eldest son of Thomas Farmer, and of Joanna Farmer, (née Clark). His father was in business as a pastry cook and confectioner, but did not settle too long in any one place and so the family moved a number of times in Scotland, to Dundee, Pitlochry, Carnoustie, Perth and finally Edinburgh. Such moves did not allow Donald a settled education and at the tender age of twelve he was apprenticed to a firm of bakery engineers in Edinburgh, at a wage of half a crown a week (12$^1$/$_2$ pence) with daily hours of 6 am to 5 pm.

Being confined indoors for long periods, he joined the newly formed 12th Edinburgh Company of the Boy's Brigade, and perhaps as a result of these activities it was not long before he felt a yearning for the military life. In 1892 he presented himself at the recruiting office of the local Militia and was advised to undergo six weeks training at the Royal Scots Depot, at Glencourse Barracks, Edinburgh. On completing his 'ordeal by fire', he returned to the recruiting office but to his dismay was told to return when he was a few months older. Not to be outdone, and having determined his future he made his way to Leith Fort, was attested (aged only 14 years and ten months) and was sent to the Depot of the Queen's Own Cameron Highlanders at Inverness. He was then still under 15 years of age although he had signed on as being 18 years and one month old, and was now faced with the rigorous training of a new recruit in the Army. In those days it was a 'make or break' routine that bordered on ill treatment, with no chance to complain and only the hardiest recruits surviving. But this toughening process, even at such an early age, enabled his character to mature. After six months training he was posted to Malta to join the 1st Battalion of the Regiment in September 1892.

Whilst here, he was frequently questioned about his age but was able to respond with a satisfactory answer. The following year he gained promotion to lance corporal, showing the commitment he applied to his chosen career. After service in Malta until 1895,the Battalion moved to take up garrison duties at Gibraltar and there followed a long period of guards, drills, and working parties that offered little in the way of excitement. On 1 April 1897 a group of long established men were sent home to form a second battalion, and this provided an opportunity for those remaining to seek further promotion to handle the newly arriving replacements. He was asked to re-engage, and for this received a bounty of £3, and was promoted to corporal.

After a period of leave at home, the Battalion moved off to Cairo, and this was the start of active service, for they were to be part of the Infantry Brigade that was to take revenge on the Mahdi for the death of General Gordon in the Sudan. This was a campaign to test the fittest, with long marches in the heat of the day, incessant flies, and problems with drinking water. They marched 100 miles to Berber in four days and camped at Darmali in preparation for the first clash with the Dervishes at the battle of Atbari on 8 April 1898, when the Brigade gained great success. After consolidating their position they had to wait for the level of the River Nile to rise sufficiently so that supplies and two gunboats could be transported for the impending battle of Omdurman that began on 2 September. The British troops, supported by troops from Egypt and Sudan, successfully routed the enemy and ended the rule of the tyrants. Years afterwards, Farmer remarked that 'as they were all fanatics, we just had to exterminate them'. There were further skirmishes before the campaign was ended and the Brigade returned to Cairo.

Dysentery had been rife among the troops and it was some time before many of them were fit enough to resume duty. The South African War began on 2 October 1899, and the 1st Battalion the Camerons were duly sent south, arriving in East London, South Africa, in February 1900. The war had then lasted for almost four months, and the Boers had met with some success largely due to their knowledge of the land and their use of parties of sharpshooters who created havoc with the formal military tactics of the British. Donald Farmer became a member of the Mounted Infantry of the regiment, created out of a need to pursue the Boer raiders who were excellent horsemen. The enemy was a highly effective force lacking nothing in combative skills, operating in relatively small units and using the terrain to great advantage. They were well-armed, enabling them to cause great damage to the units of the British Army. During one of their raids on the camp of General Clement at Nooitgedacht, Lt James Walter Sandilands of the Cameron Highlanders, with 15 men, went to the assistance of a picket which was heavily engaged, most of the men having been killed or wounded. The enemy who were hidden by trees opened fire on the party at a range of about 20 yards, killing two and wounding five, including Lt Sandilands. Sergeant Donald Farmer, without any hesitation, went to the seriously wounded officer in full view of the enemy, and although the officer was completely helpless he carried him away to a place of comparative safety, all the time under heavy and close fire. Farmer then rejoined his men in the firing line, but they were heavily outnumbered and were eventually taken prisoner. The Boers kept them for a few days and then set them down at Rustenburg, leaving them to make their own way to Pretoria some 80 miles away.

Lt Sandiland's life had been saved by the unselfish and fearless action of Donald Farmer who was deservedly awarded the Victoria Cross which was presented to him on 15 August 1901 by the Duke of York, at the town of Pietermaritzburg, on the occasion of a visit by the Duke and Duchess to the Province. It was particularly special for Donald Farmer, for two officers and 50 men of his battalion had been selected as part of the escort for the Royal visitors, and they were able to witness the first presentation of the coveted award to a Cameron Highlander.

The Battalion returned home to Fort George, Inverness in 1902 for a spell of home service, during which Farmer captained the regimental football team. In 1903 he married Helen Hall Menzies, the daughter of Archibald Newton Bonnar, of Biggar in Lanarkshire. Lt Sandilands was his best man. Sergeant and Mrs. Farmer had a family of three daughters and a son by the time he went to war in 1914.

**The Liverpool Scottish Football Club**
**Farmer front row far right**

Donald Farmer was promoted to Colour Sergeant in 1905, and the Battalion moved to the Royal Barracks, Dublin; two years later they were posted to Tidworth, on Salisbury Plain. In 1909 Farmer made the move which was to bring him within the scope of this book, for a position became available for a Colour Sergeant Instructor to the 10th (Scottish) Battalion of the King's (Liverpool) Regiment. He saw this as an ideal opportunity to complete his 21 years' service in a place where he was more likely to obtain civilian employment afterwards. This was rather a shrewd move and was ultimately to be of mutual benefit to the city and to Farmer himself. He became Company Sergeant Major and in 1914 was discharged with that rank as a pensioner. He then took his first job out of uniform, with W & R Jacob Limited, biscuit manufacturers of Long Lane, Aintree, Liverpool. Within months of starting he was called up for duty on the outbreak of war.

The 1/10th Battalion (Scottish) The King's (Liverpool) Regiment, under the command of Lieut. Colonel W. Nicholl was mobilised and sent to King's Park, Edinburgh, and there commenced training for war. Donald Farmer, who had reenlisted as a private with 'C' Company, was soon promoted Sergeant and within weeks to the rank of Regimental Sergeant Major. The Battalion moved to Tunbridge Wells, and soon they were aboard the steamship *Maidan* (Thos. Brocklebank) *en route* for France and Flanders, on 1 November 1914. They were the first Territorial battalion of the King's to leave England, and were assigned to the 9th Brigade. On 27 November the Brigade took over the front line trenches east of Mount Kemmel and west of Wytschaete, and the section occupied was only 40 yards from the enemy line. Donald Farmer remarked that this was something of an eye-opener for him: it was his first experience of trench warfare. The first winter in France in the line was an abomination for all who were there. The cold, the wet, and the mud surrounded their very existence and restricted the movement of both sides, mainly due to sniping and bombing raids.

The Battalion moved into the Ypres Salient to prepare for the battle of Hooge, and were fortunate enough to miss the first German gas attack. On 16 June 1915 they tasted their first full scale action at Bellewarde, a leap-frogging assault on the German trenches which gained little more than 1,000 yards of enemy trench, but at a heavy cost. The Battalion lost 21 officers out of 24, one of the survivors being their Medical Officer, Noel Chavasse. Farmer described Chavasse as 'the bravest man I know'. It was just after this battle that Donald Farmer was given a commission as Lieutenant Quarter-master and appointed to the 2nd Battalion, then at Ashford in Kent. They moved to Canterbury, and while he was here he was granted compassionate leave owing to his wife's serious illness in Liverpool. During his leave he was given the task of forming the 2nd Battalion West Lancashire Division Cyclists Company, and despite his domestic worries managed to fill the requirement by recruiting a full muster of 150 men in six weeks.

He returned to the 2nd Battalion at Canterbury, to find that his job as Quartermaster had been filled in error, but he was given the position of Adjutant and was promoted Captain on 1 June 1916. The following year he was back in France, in the Bois Grenier sector south of Armentières, and for most of the time was engaged in patrol activities, the lines being under heavy bombardment from the Germans. The winter was to bring the dreaded mud again and almost everywhere activity stagnated. In the spring of 1918, the 2nd Battalion was disbanded and merged with the 1st Battalion. Donald Farmer was given command of a cadre unit to help train the Americans and selected 60 officers, NCOs and other ranks, and they were posted to a chateau near Boulogne. After this exercise had been completed he was posted to a Divisional Reception Camp, where battle-weary troops were treated and retrained to take over relief duties in the line. He was promoted to Lieut. Colonel in July 1919 and was in charge of the camp in Brussels dealing with troops coming home for demobilisation. Later he was appointed to the Navy and Army Canteen Board, and in 1921 was retired.

He had hoped to return to Jacob's Biscuits but obviously did not want to go back to a low paid job. He became a military representative with the Navy, Army and Air Force Institute, a job which kept him in uniform and in touch to some extent with Army matters and his colleagues. This job however, did not last, for once the home bases had been brought up to standard he became surplus to requirements. He then became a representative with a firm of flour millers, then after a couple of years was involved in sports outfitting. In 1925, he became a representative with Younger's Brewery. He worked from home as the area representative, for the only premises owned by Youngers in Liverpool was the Clock Inn in London Road, which was well-situated just round the corner from the Fraser Street HQ of the 10th Battalion 'Liverpool Scottish'. No doubt the drill nights of this famous group of 'Terriers' were always something special in their adopted Regimental Mess, presided over by Lieut. Colonel Donald Farmer VC.

The Second World War came and although he tried to involve himself in the local Home Guard, the air raids on Merseyside made it so difficult for him to maintain his business links that he just could not cope with both. He was also near retirement age and really had seen enough of war. In Liverpool he lived at various times at addresses in Duddingston Avenue, Waverley Road, Bristol Road and finally at 165 Greenhill Road.

He was the kind of man who readily made friends, all of whom had the greatest respect for him. In 1950, at the regimental reunion in Inverness, he met again Major General J.W. Sandilands CB, DSO,CMG, the former young lieutenant whose life he had so courageously saved 50 years earlier. Six years later on 23 December 1956, this remarkable man died at the age of 79 years. His wife died in 1968 aged 91 years.

Farmer's funeral took place on Friday 28 December 1956, at Anfield Cemetery, the service being conducted by the Rev.A.A.Bell, the minister of St. Andrew's Church, Rodney Street, Liverpool. The coffin, draped in the Union Jack upon which were placed his twelve medals, was borne by eight serving Warrant Officers and Sergeants of the 1st Battalion of the Liverpool Scottish. At the end of the service W.B. Gardner, a former Pipe-Major in the Battalion, played the lament 'The Death of the Chief', and this was followed by the march 'Lieut. Colonel D.D.Farmer VC' which Bill Gardner had composed in 1950 in honour of the great man.

Lieutenant Colonel Donald Dickson Farmer VC, was proud of his family, and of his Regiment and all its traditions, and it was largely through his efforts that the Regimental Association was formed in 1930. He was its Chairman from the very start and retained that position until his death. He was cremated at Anfield Crematorium and in recent years a brass inscribed plaque to his memory has been affixed to a tree in the cemetery. His Victoria Cross is displayed at the

Regimental Museum of the Queen's Own Highlanders at Fort George, Inverness. In addition to his Victoria Cross, Farmer's medals (below) included the Queen's Sudan Medal; Queen's South Africa Medal with 4 clasps; the King's South Africa Medal with 2 clasps; the 1914 Star, British War Medal (1914-1920), and Victory Medal; George VI Coronation Medal; Queen Elizabeth II Coronation Medal; Meritorious Service Medal; and Army Long Service and Good Conduct Medal.

\* \* \* \* \* \*

**Captain Donald Farmer MC** was the only son of Donald Dickson Farmer VC, and was born in Rock Ferry on 26 July 1910. He was educated at Alsop High School, Queen's Drive, Walton, where he became a member of the school Cadet Corps, and was one of the first members of 'D' Company, Liverpool Scottish Cadets in 1925. The following year he joined the band of the Liverpool Scottish, and was to serve as a member of the Territorials through the ranks until posted as Company Sergeant Major in the Highland Light Infantry. He was commissioned in the field in November 1944, and promoted T/Captain in June 1945. He was awarded the Military Cross for gallantry on 24 March 1945. His citation was as follows:

*During the early hours of 24th March 1945, and while still dark, Lieutenant Farmer's platoon was the leading platoon of 'B' Company, Highland Light Infantry whose task was to clear about half a mile of the River Rhine Bund from South to North. This line was strongly held by two enemy Parachute Companies and consisted of several skilfully dug-in Spandau positions. Whenever our troops made any movement, they were greeted by a hail of fire. Our casualties mounted quickly and progress became almost impossible. At this juncture Lieutenant Farmer, realising the urgency of getting the Bund clear, decided to go forward alone by using smoke grenades and his Sten gun. The first post required a dash of about 100 yards which Lieut. Farmer accomplished successfully. On arrival he finally eliminated the post of eight Germans with "36" grenades. His platoon, which was now only the size of a strong section, came up and joined him. A similar situation with the next German post arose. Lieut. Farmer again captured this post single-handed. After this episode his platoon, which had previously been somewhat disheartened by casualties, cleared some other posts with Lieutenant Farmer leading. After clearance of this part of the Rhine Bund it enabled the commencement of both bridge building over the river and the LVT ferry service.*

*This officer's leadership and gallantry contributed largely to the successful starting of these vital tasks. Throughout this action, Lieut. Farmer's personal gallantry was an inspiration to his men. The eventual successful clearance of this strongly held area was undoubtedly due to this Officer's total disregard for danger, perseverance under heavy and continual fire and above all, great example to the men of his Platoon.*

Having served throughout the war, Donald Farmer Junior was demobilised in November 1945, and when the Territorials were reformed he relinquished his commission and rejoined the Liverpool Scottish as a Company Sergeant-Major, and in this capacity was a participant in the restoration of old traditions in the Sergeants' Mess.

He had been employed at the Liverpool Branch of W.T. Glover & Co. Ltd. whose office was in South Castle Street, and returned after demobilisation to later become the manager for Merseyside and North Wales. In 1959, he was made redundant when the firm was taken over by the giant BICC organisation, and he and his wife moved south where he took employment with Pirelli General as a sales clerk in Southampton, staying until his retirement. He had always been interested in sport, taking after his father, for both were talented amateur footballers. Donald and his wife lived in the south of England until his death in 1995 in Winchester, Hampshire.

# (John) *Vincent* Holland
# VC

**B**orn on 19 July 1889 at Athy, County Kildare, Ireland, John Vincent Holland was the eldest son of the local veterinary surgeon, John Holland MRCVS, and of Katherine (née Peppard). The family home was the Model Farm, Athy. Holland's father, who came from Castlecomer, County Kilkenny, was a University Gold Medallist and one time President of the Royal Veterinary Society of Great Britain and Ireland. John Holland Senior died in January 1918, and his wife died aged 87 in 1953. They had eight children, five sons and three daughters, the last of whom died in 1987.

Vincent Holland was educated at Clongowes Wood College at Naas, County Kildare, and from there obtained a place at Liverpool University where he studied

**John Vincent Holland VC**

veterinary science. The academic life and the prospect of being a country 'vet' did not really appeal to him and he left University. His father paid his fare to the Argentine to work on the railways, at the time a fairly popular venture. The 'great outdoors' offered an opportunity to indulge in plenty of riding and Vincent was an accomplished horseman. He travelled extensively in South America involving himself in hunting and ranching, besides working on the railway system, which at the time was to a very large extent a British investment and under British management.

At the time of the invasion of Belgium in 1914, Vincent was in Santa Fe and in his own words was 'impressed by' the resistance offered by Belgium; he decided to join the Belgian Army. If it was too late for that, he thought he might join the French Foreign Legion to continue the fight against German aggression. When England, in his opinion very belatedly, 'took up the sword on behalf of Belgium', he decided to join the British Army, returned to England and enlisted as a trooper in the 2nd Life Guards, on 2 September. In February 1915 he was granted a commission as a Second Lieutenant in the 3rd Battalion the Leinster Regiment and on arrival in France was attached to the 2nd Battalion the Royal Dublin Fusiliers. Wounded in the Second Battle of Ypres in May 1915, he was fortunate to miss the first gas attacks. After recovering from his wounds he returned to France and was attached to the 7th Battalion the Leinster Regiment as Battalion Bombing Officer. He was in action at the Battle of Loos from 25 September to 19 October 1915, an action in which the British first retaliated with the use of chlorine gas, though without any great success. In this battle the German defenders took a terrific toll on the British, who suffered some 60,000 casualties including three major generals killed, and the trench warfare was some of the fiercest fought in the whole of the war. Before winter had reduced operations to a minimum, Vincent Holland took part in the fighting at Hulluch and on the Somme.

It would appear that in early 1916 he returned to the 3rd Battalion the Leinsters which was based at Victoria Barracks, Cork. The Battalion was a reserve unit, used for the newly enlisted to be trained and for those who had recovered from wounds to be allocated to units requiring reinforcements. From here Holland moved to Kingstown to sail on 14 July, *en route* yet again for the battlefields of France.

On 1 July the Battle of the Somme began. It was probably the most disastrous start to any campaign. Despite months of preparation for the attack, the strength of the German positions had been totally underestimated. Again the British were faced with horrendous casualties, over 60,000 on the first day, a day on which some of the bloodiest ever fighting took place. Nine Victoria Crosses were awarded on that day, six of them posthumously. Vincent Holland rejoined the 7th Battalion which was moving up to a position opposite the village of Guillemont, a focal point in the attack. By this time the village had already been subjected to several major attempts at capture involving indescribable slaughter. Each attack was repulsed from the heavily-invested German positions.

The 7th Battalion moved into the line in the latter part of August, the troops all keyed up for their assault, from the Trones Wood area, on this seemingly impregnable obstacle. On 3 September Vincent Holland made his own individual mark in military history. He was known to his contemporaries in the Officers' Mess as 'Tinbelly Holland', a reference to his enlistment as a trooper in the Life Guards, but his gallantry was to earn him the complete respect of his comrades in arms. He demonstrated most conspicuous bravery, during a heavy engagement when, not content with bombing hostile dugouts within the objective, he fearlessly led his bombers through their own artillery barrage and cleared a great part of the village in front. He started out with 26 bombers and finished up with only five, after capturing some 50 prisoners. This gallant action undoubtedly broke the spirit of the enemy, and saved many casualties when the battalion made a further advance. He was far from well at the time, and later had to go into hospital. Of his 26 companions, two were awarded a Distinguished Conduct Medal, six a Military Medal and one was recommended for a commission.

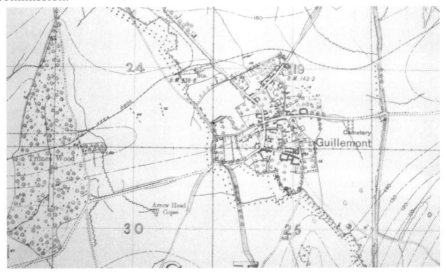

Vincent Holland earned his Victoria Cross at Guillemont on the same day as Sergeant David Jones, of the 12th Battalion of The King's (Liverpool) Regiment, who was also taking part in the attack, but who was awarded his Cross posthumously (see *Liverpool Heroes* Book 1). [Guillemont was the scene of the valour of other VC winners, including Gabriel George Coury VC (08.08.1916) and Noel Godfrey Chavasse VC (09.08.1916), both of whom feature in Liverpool Heroes Book 1.]

Like many others, Holland was quick to point out that his award was in recognition of the bravery and efforts of his men. In a speech to Athy Urban District Council in February 1917 he said: 'I would betray an unspoken trust and be unworthy of this Cross did I not now and always bear witness to the fact that the proud honour I am fortunate enough to bear could never have been mine but for the fidelity and extraordinary gallantry of the men I commanded'.

Holland was the first VC of his Regiment in the First World War, and shortly afterwards was promoted Captain. He had already been Mentioned in Dispatches, and had received the Parchment of the 16th Irish Division.

Vincent was married on 15 January 1917 to Frances Grogan, the youngest daughter of Joseph Grogan JP of the Manor House, Queenstown, and of Rossleague. Joseph Grogan's business interests included the servicing of Royal Naval vessels during the Great War when Queenstown (now Cobh) was a significant RN base for the war against U-boats in the Atlantic and Bay of Biscay. After his marriage, Vincent was appointed Staff Instructor, 16 Officer Cadet Battalion, at Kinmel Park, North Wales.

With the disbandment of the Leinster Regiment, on 27 November 1919 Holland joined the 9th Lancers in India. This position enabled him to enjoy and demonstrate his horsemanship, particularly on the polo field, and after brief service in India he was on the move again, this time to the Colonial Service in Kenya. By this time he had been appointed Major.

Vincent had two sons, who because of his absence abroad were largely brought up by his wife Frances, the family home then being at 34 Elm Road, Seaforth, Merseyside. His sons, Niall and Norman, were sent to Penryn Preparatory School, in Edgbaston, Birmingham, under the auspices of the Burke Trust. Niall went on to the Royal Military College, Sandhurst, and then into the Indian Army, where he subsequently attained the rank of Major. He was awarded the Military Cross posthumously, being killed while in action with the Mahratte Light Infantry in Assam on 15 June 1944.

[The citation for Niall Holland's MC was as follows:

*This officer showed exceptional powers of leadership and endurance while in command of patrols in the Kabaw Valley during 1942 and 1943. On one occasion, when ordered to carry out a feint attack on Yazoo during the monsoon he continued to carry on despite the fact that for three days he was too sick to be able to walk. During the action at Sangskaku, March 21st - 26th 1944, when his company was hard pressed, his courage and coolness under heavy fire was an example to all ranks. He was quite unperturbed throughout the action whatever the circumstances, and he was a constant source of strength to his commanding officer throughout.*

Niall was killed on 15 June 1944 aged 25 years.]

Due to the start of the Second World War, **Norman Holland** went into the Army on leaving school. He served for six years as a Gunner in the Royal Field Artillery. He saw action in Africa, Sicily, and in Europe, and having survived such gruelling service emigrated in 1947 to Australia. He settled in Tasmania and in 1949 married his fiancée, Miss K.M. Smith, of Wanstead, London. They have three sons and three daughters. Norman became a Secondary School teacher and later a lecturer at the University of Queensland, till he retired in 1987.

Vincent Holland returned from Kenya to the United Kingdom in 1936. The family left Liverpool to set up home in Colwyn Bay, and later in London. He was employed in a number of Civil Service jobs including the Passport Office and Land Settlement Department. In 1940, he returned to the Army in India but was invalided out the following year and returned to the Civil Service in the Ministry of Food.

In 1956, he and his wife emigrated to Tasmania, where Frances died four years later. Vincent twice returned to the United Kingdom for the Victoria Cross commemorative meetings in London, his last visit being in 1970. He never became involved in public affairs, but was interested as an observer, writing several articles on topical issues, ranging from animal life to military strategy. From his youth Vincent had the urge to be

**Vincent Holland and his wife Frances**

on the move. He travelled not so much to seek fame and fortune but because he was unable to settle to domestic life. His sons missed him in their formative years, and life was extremely difficult for them and indeed for his wife. In spite of his absence both boys were successful, although Niall's life was cut short by war. Both sons reached a high level of academic attainment.

John Vincent Holland died on 27 February 1975, aged 84 years, in St. John's Park Hospital, Hobart, Tasmania. He was a very sociable character who enjoyed a convivial atmosphere and the respect that was due to his great honour. Fittingly, the State of Tasmania saw him buried with full military honours. The whole proceedings were conducted with military precision, on a beautiful sunny day with 200 marching troops. Appropriate to his rank, eight Majors were coffin bearers, followed by four young officers carrying his medals. The coffin draped in the Southern Cross was borne through the streets on a gun carriage, accompanied by a scarlet clad military band, led by a motor-cycle police escort. Requiem Mass was offered in the Cathedral by the Archbishop, Dr. Gifford Young, who spoke on the life of a gallant soldier. The 'Last Salute' was fired and a bugler sounded the 'Last Post'. As the troops stood with weapons reversed John Vincent Holland VC was buried beside his wife Frances.

Vincent Holland was also awarded the Cross of the Legion of Honour by the French Government, and the Cross of St. George by the Russians. Hobart, the second oldest city in Australia, had paid its respects handsomely. There is a simple, family memorial in Cornelian Bay Cemetery, in Hobart. His Victoria Cross is not publicly held.

# *A*lexander Malins Lafone VC

**Alexander Malins Lafone VC**

A lexander Lafone was born on 19 August 1870 at 'Cressfield', 4 Crosby Road South, in the district of Waterloo, near Liverpool, to Henry Lafone and his wife Lucy, née Malins. In his research, Sid Lindsay refers to the Lafones as an 'interesting family': Alexander's father, Henry Malins Lafone, was the son of Samuel Lafone, born in 1770 or 1771 in Liverpool, who in 1841 lived with his family at Park Lodge, Lodge Lane, Liverpool. Samuel established a business as a Hide and Leather manufacturer and the Liverpool Directory of 1825 already shows him living at Park Lodge and trading as a tanner. Samuel and his wife had four sons – Alexander Ross born 1808, Alfred born 1821, Henry born 1830 and Samuel Fisher, birth year unknown. By 1851 the family, which also included at least two daughters, had moved to Almond House, Almonds Green, West Derby, Liverpool. Henry (father of Alexander) was a partner in the family business which had offices in King Street, Liverpool, and operated a tannery in Bevington Bush. Samuel Fisher Lafone, Alexander's brother, emigrated at an early age to Uruguay where he became a very successful merchant and landowner and was involved in cattle raising.

In 1851, Alexander Ross Lafone (Alexander Malins Lafone's uncle) was listed as living with his wife, Emily, with his father at Almond House and his occupation is shown as 'River Plate Merchant'. Sid Lindsay describes how Samuel Fisher Lafone in 1845 purchased from the British Government a part of the East Island of the Falkland Islands. Within a couple of years, Samuel experienced some difficulties (presumably financial) in the Falklands and his brother, Alexander Ross, was obliged to come to his rescue. Together they set up the Falkland Islands Trading Company. To this day, the area of East Island is known as Lafonia. In 1861 Alexander Ross, described as a merchant in hides, and his wife were living in Thingwall Hall, Storeton on the Wirral.

Alfred, by 1861, was living with his wife, four young children and their two servants, in Hastings. His wife was born in Bermondsey and his children in Camberwell, which suggests that Alfred left Liverpool for Southern England in the 1850s.

Henry, the fourth of the sons, was the father of Alexander Malins Lafone VC. Henry's first wife died shortly after their marriage and in 1861 he lived at the Royal Waterloo Hotel, Bath Street, Great Crosby, a widower with his young daughter, Lillian. In early 1863, he married Lucy, daughter of David Malins, of Edgbaston, Birmingham. By 1871, they had returned from Birmingham and were living at 4 Crosby Road South, Liverpool, by which time they had four young children – three daughters, Ella, Lucy Beatrice and Hilda, and two sons, Henry Malins born 1867 and Alexander Malins. The family moved to live at Knockholt, Kent in the 1870's, and in 1891 Henry Pownall Malins Lafone, Alexander's older brother, was a clergyman in Ambleside, possibly as vicar of St Mary's Parish Church.

Alexander Malins Lafone was educated at Dulwich College and then studied for two years at the Electrical Engineering Institute, South Kensington, his family having moved to live at Phoenix House, Alleyne Park, Camberwell, London. For eighteen months he was employed in the workshops of Marshall and Sons, Gainsborough, Lincolnshire.

Alexander took up an appointment with the Jokai Tea Company in Assam, India, as Assistant Manager and Engineer, in 1894, and three years later joined his father's business, Butler's Wharf Limited, in London. On 28 December 1899 he joined the Montgomeryshire Yeomanry and was soon on his way to South Africa where he served with some distinction in actions against the Boers. During action in the Transvaal, west of Pretoria, on 18 August 1900 he was wounded in the right eye and was returned to England in December of that year.

He received the Queen's Medal and three clasps, and on 14 August 1901 was given a commission in the 1st County of London Middlesex Yeomanry. On 14 July 1902 he was promoted Captain and on 11 August 1911 to the rank of Major. Throughout his service years he had also held directorships with a number of companies, and was a partner in the firm of F.A. Roberts & Co. of Leadenhall Street, London.

At the outbreak of war in 1914 he was serving with his regiment in Egypt, and was in action in the Dardanelles Campaign. Evacuated to Egypt at the end of that tragic episode, his regiment was reformed and moved to Palestine to fight the Turks and Arabs there. At Beersheba, on 27 October 1917, Lafone earned the highest award for gallantry:

*For most conspicuous bravery, leadership, and self sacrifice, when holding a position for over seven hours against vastly superior forces. All this time the enemy was shelling his position heavily, making it very difficult to see. In one attack, when the enemy charged his flank, he drove them back with heavy losses. In another charge they left fifteen casualties within twenty yards of his trench, one man who reached his trench, being bayoneted by Major Lafone himself. When all his men, with the exception of three, had been hit, and the trench he was holding was so full of wounded that it was difficult to move and fire, he ordered those who could walk to move to a trench that was slightly in the rear, and from his own position maintained a most heroic resistance. When finally surrounded and charged by the enemy he stepped into the open and continued the fight until he was mortally wounded and fell unconscious. His cheerfulness and courage were a splendid example to his men, and by his leadership and devotion he was able to maintain his position, which he had been ordered to hold at all costs.*

His Colonel wrote: ' He is deeply mourned by his officers and men, and his squadron is inconsolable. Everybody loved him, and his loss is one it is quite impossible to replace'. Another stated: 'He was one of the most selfless men that ever lived, and had his life been not what it was he would not have been able to show the enduring bravery and....absolute self-sacrifice which won for him the Victoria Cross. It was not won by one swift deed of courage in the heat of a charge'.

Such comments only serve to tell us a little of this very remarkable man, but little else is known about him. Alexander Malins Lafone was 47 years old when he was awarded his VC, placing him among the older recipients. He remained a bachelor and when at home in this country lived with his parents at Court Lodge, Knockholt. His elder brother, Henry Pownall Malins Lafone, eventually became Archdeacon of Furness, having been the vicar of St. George's Church, Barrow in Furness. The descendants of the Lafones in South America are widely distributed in Uruguay and the Argentine, and are still very influentially connected.

**Lafone's grave in Beersheba War Cemetery**

Interestingly, Dulwich College boasts 4 Victoria Cross winners, including Gordon Campbell VC, who by coincidence features prominently in the stories of two other Merseyside Victoria Cross holders, namely the two Royal Navy officers Charles George Bonner VC and Ronald Neil Stuart VC (*Liverpool Heroes Book 1*).

**Park Lodge, Sefton Park Road, home of the Lafone family 1820-1845**

# $\mathcal{F}$rank Lester VC

B orn on 18 February 1896 at West View, Huyton, near Liverpool, Frank was the second son of John and Ellen Lester. His father was in business as a market gardener. When Frank was still a baby the family moved to live in Hoylake, Wirral. The 1901 Census shows the family consisting of John (born 1868), his wife Ellen (born 1871), his mother Elizabeth (born 1846), Edwin (born 1894 at Huyton), Frank (born 1896 at Huyton) and Lucy Cole Lester (born 1901 at Hoylake), all living at 28 Rudd Street, Hoylake. Frank was educated at the Hoylake National School and on leaving there in 1910 he took a job to learn joinery. In 1912 his family moved again, this time to Millers Hey in the nearby village of Irby and Frank went to work for his father in the market garden. His parents were fond of music and sang in the Hoylake Temperance and the Congregational Church choirs. They obviously passed on their interests to young Frank who became involved in the Boys' Brigade and was also known to play the organ for services and meetings of the local Methodists at Miss Dodd's farm in Irby.

**Frank Lester VC**

Frank enlisted in the Army in March 1916, and was posted to the 10th Battalion the South Lancashire Regiment and his upbringing together with his training in the Boys' Brigade enabled him to adjust readily to the discipline and drill routines. It was not long before he was promoted to the rank of sergeant-instructor, training recruits at Prees Heath, Shropshire, and at Kinmel Park,

North Wales. In June 1917 he was transferred at his own request to the Lancashire Fusiliers, and in December of that year was drafted to France with the 10th Battalion. By going overseas he relinquished his rank of sergeant-instructor and reverted to the rank of private.

Winter in the front line was a miserable affair, and activity was confined to patrols and working parties in what appeared to be oceans of mud. The massive German offensive of 1918 took a heavy toll of British lives, and Frank Lester was one of 30 survivors from more than 1000 who were completely swamped by the German advance. He did not escape unharmed, being slightly wounded in the fighting, and was sent to hospital in Rouen for treatment. He had by now been promoted to the rank of corporal and on leaving hospital returned to the United Kingdom to await another posting. After some leave he was sent to Cromer, in Norfolk and in September was again on his way to the front, this time to be part of the British offensive which was beginning to drive the Germans back beyond the lines they had overrun in March.

There can be no doubting the desperate resistance of the Germans as they tried to maintain their defensive line which was being steadily pushed back. They were determined to prevent a rout, and with the once 'impregnable' Hindenburg Line now in the hands of the Allies they were fighting for survival in the most tenacious way. The weather had not been good and there had been days of driving rain and sleet. On 12 October 1918 Corporal Frank Lester earned his Victoria Cross; he was 22 years old.

His citation was published in the *London Gazette* on 14 December 1918:

*For most conspicuous bravery and self-sacrifice during the clearing of the village of Neuvilly on October 12, 1918, when with a party of about seven men under an officer, he was the first to enter a house from the back door, and shot two Germans as they attempted to get out by the front door. A minute later a fall of masonry blocked the door by which the party had entered. The only exit into the street was under point-blank range. The street was also swept by the fire of machine-guns at close range. Observing that an enemy sniper was causing heavy casualties to a party in a house across the street, Corporal Lester exclaimed, ' I'll settle him', and, dashing out into the street, shot the sniper at close quarters, falling mortally wounded at the same instant. The gallant man well knew it was certain death to go into the street, and the party opposite was faced with the alternative of crossing the fireswept street or staying where it was and being shot one by one. To save their lives he sacrificed his own.*

Four weeks later the war was over. Many glowing tributes were paid to this 'old' Boys' Brigade boy, 'who was very bright and cheerful, helped his father with his market garden, and was a true soldier'. From his Commanding Officer:

*I have been meaning to write for some time past to tell you how proud the Battalion are and the Regiment will be of the great honour your son has brought to us. We bitterly regret that such a very gallant man should not be with us to share it, but I trust it will be of some small consolation to you to know that he will always be affectionately remembered. On behalf of the officers and men I would like to express our deep sympathy to you and all his people.*

Corporal Frank Lester VC was, like so many such heroes, of a retiring nature. Whenever he wrote home he rarely mentioned anything relating to army life so as not to add to the distress of his parents, who had been informed in July 1917, that their eldest son, Edwin, had died of heart failure following the battle of Gaza, in the Palestine campaign. At the time of Frank's death there was another son aged twelve, and two daughters.

Lester is buried in the Neuvilly Communal Cemetery Extension in France. There is a plaque to his memory in the public library at Irby, Wirral, and in the Methodist Chapel at Irby there is a bronze plaque and more recently a splendid collage was installed there, designed and presented by Denis S.A. Rose of Greasby who has diligently researched the lives of the Wirral VCs. There is also a marble plaque in the United Reformed Church in Hoylake (now closed), and Lester's name appears on the family memorial at Holy Trinity Church, Hoylake. On the War Memorial at Thurstaston Church (St Bartholomew's), appear the names of both Frank and his brother, Edwin, who died on 9 July 1917 aged 23 years and is buried in Beersheba War Cemetery, Israel.

In August 2002, Frank Lester's Victoria Cross was auctioned by Messrs Morton and Eden and purchased for £78,000 by Lord Ashcroft. It now forms part of his collection of 142 VCs. According to his book *Victoria Cross Heroes*, Lord Ashcroft has plans to put his collection on public display in the near future. Wirral Borough Council was represented at the auction, and made a successful

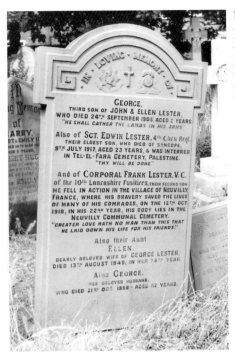

**Lester family grave at Holy Trinity Hoylake**

bid for the original wooden cross from Lester's grave in Neuvilly. The cross has been on public display in the Wirral Museum, together with a framed photograph of his mother, Ellen, taken at her Irby home upon her return from Buckingham Palace after receiving her son's Victoria Cross.

# ℛichard George Masters VC

Richard George Masters VC

R ichard George Masters was born on 23 March 1877 at 61 Everton Road, Birkdale, Southport. He was the son of David Brown Masters, and Margaret Alice Masters (née Downey). His father was a carter, a native of Birkdale, and his mother a domestic servant born in Penzance. In 1881, the family was still living at 61 Everton Road and consisted of David, Margaret and their two children, Richard George, born 1877, and Catherine born 1879. The 1891 and 1901 Censuses show them living at 4 Bury Road, Birkdale, and by 1901, in addition to Richard and Catherine, there were five other children: Louisa, born 1881, David, born 1885, Matthew, born 1888, Bessie, born 1891 and William, born 1893. Richard George was educated at Bury Road School and in 1891 was described as a cycle fitter.

In 1901 Masters married Alice Johnson and they lived at 102 Norwood Road, Southport, eventually having three children. For some time prior to August 1914 he was in the employ of a Mr. Pennington, of Birkdale, as a chauffeur.

Shortly after war was declared in 1914, Richard enlisted in the Army Service Corps – indeed all five of the Masters sons enlisted. Older than most volunteers at the time, after his initial army training he was posted as an ambulance driver, attached to 141st Field Ambulance Unit in France, serving in the forward positions of the front line. On the morning of 7 March 1917, after a bombing raid in the Somme area, Masters volunteered to go forward with a motor ambulance to an advanced dressing station located in a quarry. He made four journeys under heavy fire from enemy artillery, to clear the wounded who were virtually trapped there. His courageous action was to earn him recognition from the French Government with the award of the Croix de Guerre, presented to him by Brigadier General Edwards, at the Town Hall, Southport.

Just over twelve months later, on 9 April 1918, near Gorre, Masters earned his Victoria Cross. The citation read as follows:

> *Owing to enemy attack, communications between the 'Tuning Fork' and the town of Bethune from the Division north of the canal was cut off, and wounded could not be evacuated. The road from Gorre to the 'Tuning Fork' was reported impassable but Private R.G. Masters volunteered to get through, and after the greatest difficulty succeeded, although he had to clear the road of all sorts of debris. He made journey after journey from 1 pm. until darkness set in, over a road consistently shelled and swept with machine gun fire, and on one occasion was bombed by an aeroplane. The greater part of two hundred wounded cleared from this area were evacuated by Private Masters as his was the only car that got through between 1 pm. and 5 pm. In assisting in removing wounded from the cellars of a house he was gassed, from the effects of which he still suffering.*

Masters was a man who was dedicated to his task whether it was as a chauffeur in civilian life, or as a front line driver who was well aware of the necessity of moving the wounded from the line as quickly as possible if lives were to be saved. He had served his country in France for over three years. He was a man who took a great pride in his appearance, always carefully groomed and dressed. After the war he resumed his employment as a private chauffeur, and over the years he worked at four different places. For a time he was chauffeur to Sir George Stephenson, then the owner of the *Southport Visitor* newspaper. One can imagine the pride (or envy) of his employers, but he eventually took up employment as a driver with Southport Corporation Gas Department until his retirement.

When he returned to Southport after his award, the Town Council donated £200 towards a 'town testimonial'; a sum of £500 was eventually invested in the form of War Bonds, and his wife was presented with jewellery. In addition, it is said, he was presented with a lifetime contract for admission to the Neville Street Picture House!

He was a keen sportsman and between 1898 and 1900 was one of the country's foremost cyclists, better known locally as George Masters, of the Southport Harriers. He held the Liverpool District National Cycling Union Championship four times, the Centenary Shield four times and on a tandem with W. Birtwhistle had established world records for the quarter mile and half mile. He even won a 100 yard sprint in the Division (Scratch) Running Race and Veterans Handicap in 1916, at a base sports event.

Masters was an active and staunch supporter of the Royal Army Service Corps Association, and was Life President of the Southport Branch. He died at his home, 35 Palmerston Road, Southport, on 4 April 1963, aged 86 years, four days after celebrating his birthday. He had been ill for a few months but up till then had regularly taken a five-mile walk with his Cairn terriers, giving most of his acquaintances the impression that he was a much younger man.

The Water Transport section of the RASC was responsible for the provision of vessels as Range Target Towing launches, General Service launches and Range Safety launches, to cater for artillery practice in coastal areas. In the early 1970s, the RAF Establishment at Farnborough acquired the services of an ex-naval inshore minesweeper for some highly important research work. This ship was named *Richard George Masters VC*, and Master's sister was invited to carry out the naming ceremony on HM Gun Wharf at Portsmouth. Her skipper was Captain F. Bourne who had been with the ship for some years before her renaming and had sailed many thousands of miles in her. She was subsequently paid off when her hull began to become suspect after 30 years' service.

An autographed menu from a VC Garden Party in June 1920, sold recently at auction, bears George Masters' signature, no doubt indicating that he was one of many VC winners who attended. A TA Centre at Bootle used by the Royal Logistical Corps bears his name. On 26 April 2006 a memorial service was held at his graveside in St Cuthbert's Churchyard, Churchtown, and was attended by members of the 156 Transport Regiment and John Masters, a nephew. His Victoria Cross is proudly displayed at the Headquarters of the Royal Logistical

Corps in Camberley and on 26 January 2006 an accommodation block at Sandhurst, named after Masters, was dedicated by Johnson Beharry VC, the most recent living recipient of this award. [The most recent award of the VC was made posthumously to Bryan James Budd of the 3rd Battalion the Parachute Regiment, for his bravery in Afghanistan in August 2006; the award was announced on 14 December 2006.]

**Grave of Richard George Masters VC**

# $\mathscr{P}$atrick Mylott VC

P atrick Mylott was born in 1820 at Hollymount, near Claremorris, Co. Mayo, Ireland, but other than this very little is known about this 'Liverpool hero'. It is believed that he enlisted in the 63rd Regiment (2nd Suffolk Regiment) on 18 May 1839, and then transferred to the 84th Regiment (later to become the York and Lancaster Regiment), on 1 January 1847. While serving with this regiment in India during the Mutiny, Patrick Mylott earned the nation's highest award for valour. His was the 168th Victoria Cross awarded and his citation reads:

> *For being foremost in rushing across a road, under a shower of balls, to take an opposite enclosure; and for gallant conduct at every engagement at which he was present with his regiment from the 12th July 1857, to the relief of the Lucknow garrison. Elected by the Private soldiers of the regiment.*

There is some confusion about some of the facts, but according to the VC file of Canon Lummis he is said to have been promoted to sergeant and later to ensign, but the Regimental Museum in Rotherham believes that this is unlikely, because he was illiterate and could not sign his name. On 4 December he was pensioned off after serving 21 years. Patrick Mylott received his Victoria Cross from HM Queen Victoria at an Investiture held in the Quadrangle of Windsor Castle on 4 January 1860. His pension was increased to 8¹/2d per day in 1863.

A man named William Patrick Mylott is buried in a public grave in Anfield Cemetery, Liverpool, and it is believed that this is the same man who so earned the respect of his comrades at Lucknow that they elected him for the Victoria Cross. William Patrick Mylott died on 22 December 1878, in Brownlow Hill Workhouse, Liverpool, having been taken there from his home in Duckworth Street (off Dale Street). He was obviously living in straitened circumstances for where he lived was one of a number of small courts containing overcrowded, unsanitary dwellings. It was not unusual for Irishmen who had served in the Regular army not to return home on their discharge. It is not known whether Patrick Mylott was married or remained single. In 1994, again largely due to the efforts of Sid Lindsay and Maurice Rigby, a memorial stone to William Patrick Mylott VC was erected in Anfield Cemetery. As the exact location of his grave cannot be identified, the stone bears the inscription 'within this cemetery'.

Research into the Census records show only two possible entries for Patrick Mylott living in Liverpool. In 1841, Patrick Mylett (not Mylott), born about 1811 in Ireland, is shown as a lodger living in Hackins Hey, Liverpool. In 1851, Patrick Mylett, a corn porter born in County Mayo in about 1816, was living as a lodger with a family called O'Donnell, also from Mayo, at 47 Cheapside, Liverpool. Any further information about Patrick or William Patrick Mylott/Mylett would be welcome.

The whereabouts of Mylott's Victoria Cross are unknown.

**Mylott's headstone at Anfield Cemetery Liverpool**

# $\mathscr{T}$homas Patrick Neely
## VC MM

Thomas Neely was born on 26 August 1897 at 13 Tabor Street (off Brighton Street), Poulton-cum-Seacombe, Wallasey, the only son of James Herbert Neely and Mary Agnes (née Egan). His father worked as a journeyman gasfitter, but was unable to find regular employment and for some years had worked as a casual general labourer. While Thomas was still young the family moved across the Mersey to live at 91 Claudia Street, Walton, Liverpool. He was educated at St. Francis de Sales School in Hale Road, Walton.

On leaving school he went to work at J. Bibby & Sons Ltd. seed crushers, soap and cattle food manufacturers in Great Howard Street. He was small and stocky and

**Thomas Neely VC**

a very energetic character and it was no surprise to his workmates when he enlisted in the Bantam Battalion of the Cheshire Regiment in September 1914. He was just 17 years of age.

Details of his war service are sketchy, but he seems to have been keen and, in spite of his tender years, a very capable soldier. On completing his training he was transferred to the King's Own Lancaster Regiment. He was very much in the front line action in France and was wounded twice. In 1918 Neely took part in the action which was to win him the Military Medal, the award of which was announced in the *London Gazette* on 16 July that year. He was duly allowed extra leave at home, mainly because he had spent such a long time in the front line trenches. He returned to the front on 26 August and was promoted to full corporal. His Company Commander was so impressed with this young man's qualities of leadership and skill as a soldier that he tried to persuade him to apply for a commission, but Neely was quite happy as an NCO and his Battalion CO was convinced that he was of more use in this role where he was close to his comrades, particularly at this critical stage of the war. He was soon promoted to lance sergeant.

In September 1918 the new British offensive was launched, and the 8th Battalion the King's Own Lancasters were located to the south west of Cambrai, at a place called Flesquières. This village, standing close to the Canal du Nord, had been the scene of bitter fighting in November 1917 and had been retaken by the enemy in their Spring offensive of 1918. It was a key position in protecting the heavily barricaded Hindenburg Line, a system of fortified trench works stretching across the open land. This was thought to be the Germans' last line of defence and as such it was almost impregnable, every inch of ground held by the enemy in front of it being contested fiercely. The British attack however was such that it began to roll the German front line back, slowly and painfully, as the enemy made its last desperate stand. It seemed to be the culmination of all the horrors that had been going on for the past four years. Thomas Neely was a member of the 15th Platoon of 'D' Company, 8th Battalion, and on 27 September they were on the outskirts of the village attempting to drive the Germans from their advanced trenches.

The *London Gazette* of 14 December 1918 stated:

> *For most conspicuous bravery during operations at Flesquières on September 27, 1918. His company was held up during the advance by heavy machine-gun fire from a flank. Corporal Neely, realising the seriousness of the situation, at once, under point blank fire, dashed out with two men and rushed the positions, disposing of the garrisons and capturing three machine-guns. Subsequently, on two successive occasions, he rushed concrete strong points, killing or capturing the occupants. The splendid initiative and fighting spirit displayed by this gallant non-commissioned officer in dealing with a series of posts, in*

*some cases single-handed, was largely responsible for the taking and clearing of a heavily fortified and strongly garrisoned position, and enabled his company to advance 3,000 yards along the Hindenburg support line.*

The award of the VC to Neely was justly deserved, but only three days later, on 1 October 1918, he was killed in action at Romilly. He is buried at Masnieres Cemetery, to the south east of Cambrai, and there is a memorial plaque in the Regimental Chapel in Lancaster Priory Church. Although he was an only son, at the time of his death he had five sisters, and in May 1919 his mother gave birth to another son. Thomas's mother received her son's Victoria Cross from King George V and a report in the Liverpool *Daily Post & Mercury*, dated Friday 27 February 1920 read:

*Amongst those attending the Investiture by the King at Buckingham Palace, today, were Mr. and Mrs. J.H. Neely, of Claudia St., Walton, the parents of the late Corporal (Lance-Sergeant) Thomas Neely VC, MM, when Mrs. Neely received from the King the Victoria Cross that had been awarded to her son.*

*At the beginning of the week Mrs. Neely received an invitation for herself and her husband to attend at Buckingham Palace. Unfortunately, the invitation was accompanied by only one railway warrant. Mr. Neely, who is a general labourer, has been out of work for some weeks, and the possibility of raising sufficient money to pay his railway fare to London and back seemed well nigh hopeless. Needless to say, he was greatly disappointed, but by a happy inspiration he called at the Central office in Church Street, of the Comrades of the Great War Association. Here he found Mr. Hughes (the general secretary) only too ready to help him, and not only was he provided with the money to cover his expenses in accompanying his wife to Buckingham Palace, but he was assured by Mrs. Wolfenthell (the assistant secretary) that on his return work would be found for him. Mr. and Mrs Neely left Liverpool for London last night, and Mrs. Neely had with her her ten month old baby boy.*

The records show that Tom Neely's Victoria Cross is not publicly held.

[On the same day that Thomas Neely was earning his Victoria Cross at

Flesquières on the right bank of the Canal du Nord, 27 September 1918, on the left bank of the canal the 3rd Guards Brigade was fiercely battling its way towards the Hindenburg Line. Acting Lieutenant Colonel John Gort of the Grenadier Guards led his men to the north edge of Flesquières and captured German trenches yielding 200 prisoners, and in a later reconnaissance accompanied by his servant he was to earn the Victoria Cross for conspicuous gallantry when his servant was mortally injured by an enemy shell. John Gort (Lord Gort), was to become a Field Marshal and was the Commander-in-Chief of the British land forces in France, 1939 to 1940. He died in 1946.]

# *G*eorge Edward Nurse
## VC

George Edward Nurse was born on 14 April 1873 at Enniskillen, Co. Fermanagh, Ireland. He was the son of Charles and Jane Nurse. It is thought that his father, who was born in Middlesex, was a regular soldier stationed in Ireland and that when George was very young Charles left the Army and took a position as manager of the Cobo Hotel, Cobo Bay, Guernsey. The Census returns for 1881, 1891 and 1901 show Charles, a hotel keeper, living at the Cobo Hotel. In 1881, he was living with his second wife, Jessie, and his two sons, Alfred born 1867 in Bermuda and George, born 1873 in Enniskillen. It is strange that one of Charles's sons, Alfred, should have been born in Bermuda. In 1901, bachelor George Edward Nurse is shown as living in Southill Barracks, Chatham.

**George Edward Nurse VC**

George took a course of higher education at the Chamberlain Academy, Guernsey, and at the age of eighteen decided on his career by enlisting in the Royal Artillery, London, on 6 January 1892 at St. George's Barracks. He served in London until May 1897, when the 66th Battery, Royal Field Artillery was transported to South Africa to fight the Boers. In command of the Battery was Major W. Foster, serving under Colonel Long, and the Brigade was commanded by Brigadier General Hildyard. In December 1899, at Colenso, George Nurse won his Victoria Cross.

On December 15th 1899, Colonel Long with the 14th and 66th Batteries of the Royal Field Artillery, had pressed forward to drive the Boers from their trenches along the banks of the Tugela river, expecting to be supported by reinforcements. Because of the deadly fire that was directed upon him he was forced to retire, leaving many dead and wounded behind him and also twelve

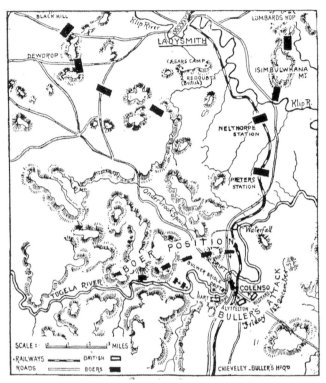

**Map showing the Boer positions on December 15 1899**

guns, standing ready for use with their breech-blocks still in them. A few of the drivers and horses who were left alive made their escape to a nearby donga (a narrow, deep ravine), some 500 yards behind the guns. The space between the donga and the guns was swept by shell as well as rifle fire, so intense that one poor gunner sustained 64 bullet wounds. Volunteers were called for in the donga to try to save the guns, and George Nurse was one of these, together with several officers and drivers. Captain Congreve, of the Rifle Brigade, who was in the donga, helped to limber up one of the guns, and in doing so was wounded in the leg and was severely grazed on the elbow and shoulder. He took shelter, but went out again to assist Lieutenant F.H.S. Roberts (son of Lord Roberts), who had fallen, badly wounded in three places. During all of this, Corporal George Nurse had been part of the action as the enemy's unceasing fire raked the ground around them. He had managed to secure some loose horses, and while Lieutenant Roberts held his horse, Nurse hooked the other horses to the limbers. Through the terrible fire they set out towards the guns but Lieutenant Roberts was shot. When they reached the guns through a tornado of bullet and shell fire, they found one gun had the spade clamping gear jammed. George Nurse ran to another gun and together with Captain H.N. Schofield managed to limber it up. Nurse then went back to the other gun, and having found the pin, limbered it up by himself.

Considering the effort involved in trying to move one of the guns, a very tricky exercise even for trained men and horses in ideal conditions, one can be appreciate the difficulties faced in this terrible situation. The limber, which carried the ammunition for the gun, was a box on wheels drawn by a team of six horses. The gun, which was itself mounted on large wheels, had to be manhandled into position and the trail (the long tail at the back of the gun) had to be attached to the back of the limber. The whole cumbersome articulated vehicle could then be towed to where it was wanted, the gunners riding postillion (riding on the near side horses) to steer the gun on its way. On the parade ground such movements were always difficult but on a battlefield often suicidal for if a horse was shot or stumbled and fell, particularly at speed, the whole contraption could come to a complete standstill and the crew abandoned to their fate. Since the gunners sat upright on their horses and their speed was governed by ground conditions, they were always extremely exposed to the fire from rifle and machine gun. In the circumstances pertaining at Colenso, their actions were tantamount to suicide.

George Nurse fought through almost the whole four colonies in South Africa from Durban in the east to the relief of Mafeking in the north west. He was decorated with the Victoria Cross by General Sir Redvers Buller VC, at Ladysmith, Natal, on 18 March 1900. He rose to be a Battery Sergeant Major and received the Ladysmith and Transvaal Clasps. In 1910 he received his Long Service and Good Conduct Medals. He left the army in 1913, having completed 21 years' service, but was recalled at the outbreak of war in 1914 and in September 1915 was commissioned as a temporary second lieutenant. His experience was used during the war in the training of artillerymen. He ended the war as a temporary captain.

George married a girl from Kilkenny, Kathleen Augustine Sweeney, in Kensington, London in 1904. They had one son, Charles Patrick Colenso Nurse, born on 26 June 1909.

At some time after the Great War, George worked for the cleaning department of the Liverpool Customs House, and it seems likely that any record of his service was lost when the Customs House was bombed in an air raid. In the 1920s the family lived at 5 Westminster Terrace, off Botanic Road, Liverpool and later at 125 Botanic Road, but George's wife died in the late 1930s and he moved to 15, Crosfield Road off Durning Road, Liverpool, where

**Sid Lindsay with members of Nurse's family at Allerton Liverpool**

he lived with a Mr. Harry Meakin, a gas worker, and his wife. George lived here until 25 November 1945, when he fell ill and died in Broadgreen Hospital aged 73 years.

He is buried in Allerton Cemetery, C of E Section 2G/608, but for many years his grave was unmarked. On 13 December 1963 members of 26 Regiment, Royal Artillery, performed a simple ceremony at the frost-covered grave and laid a wreath. There have been no other such ceremonies and the grave lay completely neglected.

On 23 February 1973 in the *Daily Telegraph*, there appeared the following item:

### BOER WAR FOREBEAR

*At least one member of the Royal Corps of Signals contingent which mounts guard at Buckingham Palace for the next fortnight can boast impeccable military antecedents. Staff Sergeant Charles George Colenso Nurse is grandson of the Boer War V.C. Corporal George Edward Nurse.*

*He owes his unusual third Christian name to his grandfather's part in the battle of Colenso Bridge in December 1899, during the early stages of the advance to relieve Ladysmith. Corporal Nurse with four comrades, including the only son of Lord Roberts who was killed in the action, braved a hail of shell and rifle fire in an attempt to prevent the guns from falling into enemy hands. All were awarded the Victoria Cross.*

Another interesting aspect of Nurse's award is that the Colenso battle saw the first award of a posthumous VC. Until this date, there was no provision for the Cross to be awarded to a man who was killed during the action which earned it. At some stage it had been accepted that where a man would have been considered for a Victoria Cross had he survived the action, this fact should be gazetted. Lieutenant Roberts, however, was the son of Lord Roberts VC and contrary to all normal procedures was awarded his Cross posthumously. This caused much consternation, leading to the award of other posthumous VCs to several of those who had died in earlier actions and had been gazetted. From then on, the rules were changed to provide for posthumous awards of the Victoria Cross.

**Grave of George Nurse VC at Allerton Liverpool**

## Postscript

Due to the efforts of Sid Lindsay and Maurice Rigby, Nurse's grave in Allerton Cemetery was located, and a campaign was begun to have his grave suitably marked. Sid made contact with Captain I.E.Paton, Royal Artillery, then serving with 159 (Colenso) Battery in Belize, Central America. On his return to the United Kingdom, Captain Paton set in motion the production of a War Graves Commission pattern headstone, inscribed with the Victoria Cross and the Royal Artillery badge and motto. Captain Paton also arranged a Service of Dedication at the grave on Saturday 8 April 1989. The ceremony was attended by one of George Nurse's grandsons and two great-grandsons, one of whom was an NCO then serving with 159 Battery, together with five other NCOs from the Battery. A Pipe-Sergeant from the Regiment played the lament. Captain D.C.Tanzey, Royal Artillery (V), of 213 Air Defence Battery (V), was the sole official representative from the local Territorial Force, while Joe Lynch, GC, BEM, represented the Victoria Cross and George Cross Association. Once again Sid Lindsay had spurred on efforts to ensure that a VC holder was recognised and remembered. Little attention is paid to Nurse's grave today save for an annual poppy wreath and occasional visits by members of the NCMAVC Committee, which is producing the *Liverpool Heroes* series. His Victoria Cross is displayed at the Royal Artillery Museum at Woolwich.

# Arthur Herbert Procter
## VC

**Arthur Herbert Procter VC**

Arthur Procter was born on 11 August 1890 at 55 Church Street, Bootle, Liverpool, the eldest son of Arthur Richard Procter, a bank clerk, and Ellen (née Cumpsty). His father was employed by Parr's Bank and the family lived on the bank premises situated on the corner of Church Street and Derby Road (the bank address was 55, Derby Road). Parr's Bank had a number of branches in the Liverpool area, merging with the Westminster Bank around 1919/20. There was a sister, Ethel, who was three years older than Arthur and there were two younger brothers. Arthur started at St. Mary's Church of England School in Church Street, but his father suffered from chronic ill-health and his mother died in her early thirties, so Arthur and his two younger brothers and sister were sent to Exeter to be brought up by their uncle. The Census of 1901 shows Arthur living with his uncle and aunt at 3 Elm Grove Terrace, Exeter. However the 1901 Census also shows his parents with three of their children, Ethel (b.1887), Clarence (b.1892) and Ernest (b.1898) and two visitors, living at 8 Boundary Road, Bebington, Wirral. Presumably they were well enough to look after Arthur's siblings while for some reason he was living with his father's brother in Exeter.

It is believed that due to his father's incapacity, which had cost him his job with the bank, and other family problems, Arthur was sent to Dr. Barnardo's Homes. This brought him back to Merseyside to the Home at Marford, Dibbinsdale Road, Bromborough. He completed his education there and at Port Sunlight school, then took employment as a clerk in the firm of Wilson & Co. of Temple Street, Liverpool, who were engaged in the wholesale provision and produce trade and were members of the Liverpool Produce Exchange in Victoria Street. Arthur became a familiar figure amongst the merchants. He was a friendly, amiable young man with deep religious feelings and was an ardent worker in the Sunday School and Mission at St. Paul's Presbyterian Church in Stuart Road, Tranmere. He took lodgings with Mr. and Mrs. I. Charles Codd, at 68, Derby Road, Tranmere, where Mr. Codd was in business as a pharmaceutical chemist. In addition to his church activities Arthur became a member of the Voluntary Aid Detachment of the local Red Cross Society and also trained with the St. John Ambulance Brigade where he gained certificates as a proficient first-aider.

He enlisted in November 1914, in the 5th Battalion, The King's Regiment, a Territorial Force battalion with a depot at St.Anne Street, Liverpool. The Battalion went out to France in February 1915, and eventually made its way to Bethune, later to be joined by the 1st and 7th Battalions. During an enemy bombardment of the town (an important headquarters and staging area), Arthur Procter was wounded in the arm by shrapnel and was sent to the 2nd Canadian Field Hospital at Le Touquet on 16 May 1915, returning to his unit in June. The 5th Bn of The King's was designated a Pioneer battalion with the 6th Brigade which was being reformed after the battle of Festubert, where the 1st Battalion had performed so courageously. The summer of 1915 meant that the pioneers were much in demand as preparations were made for the next offensive.

The 5th Battalion took part in the battle of Loos in September/October 1915, but as winter arrived they reverted more to their pioneer role.

In early 1916, there was further reorganisation and the 5th Battalion became part of the 165th Brigade which was entirely made up of The King's Battalions (5th, 6th, 7th and 9th). As the dreadful winter came to an end the patrol activity by both sides on the front increased. At this time, in the area of Blairville and Ficheux, Edward Felix Baxter of the 8th Battalion earned a post-humous Victoria Cross on the night of 17/18 April 1916 (see the first VC entry in this book). In the same area Private Arthur Herbert Procter gained this most coveted award for bravery. His Battalion had made careful plans to raid the enemy lines at Ficheux, plans which were to be thwarted, by the British Army's own artillery.

The attack had been arranged for 4 June 1916, and under an artillery barrage the 5th Battalion were to raid the German trenches ahead of them. A raiding party of two officers and 87 other ranks made their way cautiously over the parapet and deployed across the open land to await the conclusion of the bombardment so that they could then rush in. Unfortunately, the artillery had miscalculated the range and their initial salvoes fell amongst the Kingsmen causing terrible casualties. The raid was abandoned, but that evening Arthur Procter who was acting as a stretcher-bearer looked over the parapet and saw a movement from two men who, having been presumed dead, had been allowed to remain lying in the open until they might be removed under the cover of darkness. They were lying some 75 yards in front of the British trench and Arthur, on his own initiative, ran and crawled across the ground in full view of the enemy who subjected him to heavy rifle and machine-gun fire. He reached the two men, and in the words of his citation:

> *got them under the cover of a small bank, dressed their wounds, and, after cheering them up with a promise of rescue after dark, and leaving them with some of his clothing for warmth, he regained our trenches, again being heavily fired at. At dusk both men were brought out alive, and dispatched to hospital.*

Private Procter received his well deserved Victoria Cross from King George V, at British Headquarters, Amiens, in France, the first man to be so decorated on the battlefield. He came home on leave in August 1916, and after visiting his birthplace was taken to meet the Mayor and Mayoress of Bootle (Dr. and Mrs. James Pearson) and officials of the Borough Council. This modest man had hoped to make his visit a private one, but the nature of his act of gallantry made many take the opportunity of expressing their sincere appreciation to him in person. While he was with the Mayor there were a few moments of poignant drama as he was introduced to a middle-aged lady, who was evidently in deep grief but who tried to smile bravely through the tears. She was Mrs. Jones of Bank Road, Bootle, the mother of one of the men he had rescued, who unfortunately had since died. She thanked the hero for what he had done for her son. After the proceedings were over he called on her at her home in Bank Road, and told her how he knew her son quite well as they had lived within a stone's throw of each other and had attended a course on bombing together.

Procter was next received by the Lord Mayor of Liverpool at the 5th Battalion's Depot in St. Anne Street. Colonel McMasters, a former Commanding Officer of the 5th, introduced Arthur to Corporal Joe Tombs VC who had won his award in 1915, and who had been invited along to the reception. The Lord Mayor, in his speech, referred to the unique presentation by the King on the battlefield in the presence of the two Allied commanders, General Sir Douglas Haig and General Joffre, adding that Arthur Procter was the only man from a Territorial battalion of the Regiment to win this high distinction. From this reception he went on to the Liverpool Produce Exchange where he was given a tremendous welcome by members of the provision trade in Liverpool. He was introduced to the assembly by Mr. T.H. Nuttall who was his former manager at Wilson's. After various speeches, Arthur was presented with an inscribed gold watch and chain, a cheque for one hundred guineas and a £100 4% War Loan voucher, all subscribed by the Exchange members. On each occasion, thanking everyone for their gifts and kindness, this modest hero declared that there were many heroic deeds done at the front, but they were not rewarded because they had not been observed. He described himself as one of the lucky ones. Such was this great man's humility.

He returned to the front line in France and fought in the battle of the Somme in 1916. He was in action in the Ypres Salient in 1917 and at Arras in 1918. On demobilisation he returned to the provision trade as a salesman, and moved from Wilson's to the firm of George Wall & Co. Ltd. He had maintained an active interest in the Church and it was no great surprise when in 1925 he made plans to relinquish his work in the commercial scene to enrol at St. Aidan's College, Birkenhead, to take Holy Orders.

**Arthur and Hilda Procter during the Great War**

He was married on 23 May 1917 to Hilda May, the daughter of Mr. and Mrs. Codd, at whose home he had taken lodgings before enlisting in the Army. The ceremony took place at St. Paul's Presbyterian Church, North Road, Tranmere. They had three sons.

Arthur Procter was ordained in 1927 and became curate at St. Mary the Virgin, the Parish Church of Prescot, a church with many interesting historical connections. From here he was chosen to be Vicar of Bosley, a village not far from Congleton, in Cheshire. He moved from there in about 1933 to the Parish of St. Stephens in Hyde, Cheshire, now part of the Manchester conurbation. It was while he was here, in 1941, that he was appointed Chaplain in the Royal Air Force, and held the rank of Squadron Leader. After the war, in 1946, he was appointed Rector of St. Mary's Church, in Droylsden, also within the Manchester boundary, and remained there until 1951 when he moved to be Vicar of St. Peter's Church, in Claybrooke, a village lying between Leicester and Rugby. In 1963, he moved yet again, this time to become Vicar of St. John the Baptist Church at Bradbury, in North Devon. He retired from here in 1965 and went to live in Sheffield, where he died on 2 January 1973, aged 82 years of age.

He and his wife attended Victoria Cross Garden Parties, and he was involved in the services that were held in St. Martins-in-the-Field on behalf of the Victoria Cross Association. With Ian Fraser VC, John Molyneux VC and John Readitt VC (each of whom will feature in the *Liverpool Heroes* series) he attended the VC Reunion held at the Café Royal, London, on 7 July 1960. He enjoyed cricket and playing golf but like so many old soldiers did not like talking about the past nor particularly about himself. A kindly man, much respected wherever he went, he must have been a truly wonderful character to emerge from his rather tragic childhood and achieve all that he did.

On Saturday 19 July 1924 King George V and Queen Mary were in Liverpool for the consecration of Liverpool Cathedral. That afternoon, the King reviewed the 55th West Lancashire Territorial Division on Wavertree Playground. Arthur Procter V.C. was one of nine Victoria Cross holders present, and the King remarked that he remembered decorating him on the battlefield.

# *J*oseph Prosser VC

**Joseph Prosser VC**

Joseph Prosser was born in 1828 in Monegal, King's County (now Offaly) Ireland. No details are available concerning his parents or his childhood. On 11 January 1842 he enlisted as a boy soldier in the 2nd Battalion the First Regiment of Foot, later to become the Royal Scots Regiment. He was 14 years of age, and for the next three years trained as a potential infantryman. He served abroad, spending almost two years in Canada, followed by six months in Nova Scotia, and then from the cool northern climate the battalion moved south to spend the next 16 months in the West Indies. After a period of further duty in the United Kingdom, the battalion embarked for Cephalonia, the largest of the Ionian Islands which came under British control in 1809, and for the next 26 months they carried out their role as garrison force on the island.

In 1854, because of their location, the battalion was mobilised to become an early member of the expeditionary force to land in the Crimea, and Joseph Prosser was to experience the horrors of war in the frightful conditions of that poorly-conducted campaign. The battalion was in action at the battles of Alma, Inkerman, and in the protracted siege of Sevastapol. Casualties were high on both sides but the British suffered as many losses from disease and sickness as from actual fighting. The weather caused havoc and the allied troops, poorly equipped and badly led, suffered atrociously and were given little respite. The siege of Sevastapol lasted for twelve months, and the attempts to break it cost many British lives. While the 2nd Battalion Royal Scots were in the advanced trenches there Private Joseph Prosser earned his Victoria Cross.

The *London Gazette* of 24 February 1857 stated:

> *On 16th June 1855, when on duty in the trenches before Sevastapol, for pursuing and apprehending (whilst exposed to two crossfires) a soldier in the act of deserting to the enemy. Secondly, on 11th August 1855, before Sevastapol, for leaving the most advanced trench, and assisting to carry in a soldier of the 95th Regiment who lay severely wounded and unable to move. This gallant and humane act was performed under a very heavy fire from the enemy.*

It is somewhat ironic that his first mention concerns his catching a deserter, albeit under intense enemy fire, for on 27 April 1848, Prosser himself was posted as a deserter from his battalion and remained on the run until 13 June 1848, when he rejoined his unit. He was court-martialled and sentenced to 84 days imprisonment. The full circumstances of this escapade are not known nor are his reasons for apprehending the man who tried to desert, whose days must have been numbered anyhow because of his action.

The battalion left the Crimea and took up station on Malta where they spent the next 12 months. The Victoria Cross was presented to Prosser here. Upon his return home for duty in Britain it is not clear where he spent his leaves. He married and had two children, a boy and a girl. The battalion, with Joseph Prosser VC amongst them, next saw service on the Rock of Gibraltar as garrison troops and remained there for fourteen months before being dispatched for a spell of duty in the Far East on the China Stations where they stayed for just 12 months. In almost 17 years of service Prosser spent 10 years overseas.

As well as the Victoria Cross, Joseph Prosser held the Crimean Medal with Clasp for Sevastapol, together with the Turkish Crimean Medal. However, he was not an exemplary soldier throughout his service, his name having entered in the Defaulters' Book no less than 43 times, and he was court-martialled four times. He spent 182 days in detention, but it is fair to record that after he had been awarded the Victoria Cross there was an improvement (though not a complete conversion). The number of times his good conduct pay was forfeit and then restored reads like a regular serial, but the reasons for his errant behaviour are not apparent.

The brief file compiled by the late Canon Lummis MC, who endeavoured to cover the lives of all of the recipients of the Victoria Cross, tells us very little about Joseph Prosser VC. There are a couple of questionable matters however. One is that it is reported that Prosser became an officer in the Irish Customs service on leaving the Army, but as he was discharged as being medically unfit, it is unlikely that this would be the case. It is also reported that he was a drummer in the battalion - this is not stated on his army record - but he may well at some time in his service, if only for a short while, have tried his hand as a drummer. These are not particularly important issues.

By the early 1860s Prosser was a very sick man, having contracted chronic hepatitis while serving in Hong Kong, and he was discharged from the Army on 30 June 1863. The Medical Officer made the point that the disease had left him 'extremely delicate and emaciated' - not the best recommendation for taking up service in the Irish Customs. The Lummis Files also state that he died in 1869 or 1870, and is buried in Tipperary, Ireland. Research locally shows that this was not the case. He died on 10 June 1867, at almost 40 years of age, and was buried in Anfield Cemetery in an unmarked grave on 13 June. His occupation was shown as 'soldier' and his burial cost the princely sum of 62 pence! At the time of his death, he was living at 26b Birchfield Street, off Islington, Liverpool.

Also buried in Anfield Cemetery is **William Prosser**, a nephew of Joseph. William lived in Liverpool all of his life and no doubt this family relationship is the reason for Joseph finishing his days here in Liverpool.

**Prosser's headstone at Anfield Cemetery Liverpool**

Born in 1853 in Liverpool, William was a man with a history of bravery, like his uncle. William was a docker and lived at various times in Chaucer Street, Liverpool (1861 Census), Skirving Street, Liverpool (1871), Lambeth Road (1891) and finally in the Home for Aged Mariners, Wallasey, where he died in 1934. During his lifetime, William made no less than 36 rescues from the Leeds-Liverpool Canal and the River Mersey. He saved a total of 42 lives and was awarded the Liverpool Shipwreck and Humane Society's silver medal with an incredible 8 clasps! His first rescue, from the Canal, was when he was 11 years old and his last, from the Mersey, when he was 72 years old! In fact, one source claims that in 1927, when William would have been 75 years old, he made yet another rescue when he saved two young boys from drowning.

## *Postscript*

Although it has not been possible to find a record of Joseph Prosser's marriage, official sources show that in September 1865 the birth of Joseph William Prosser was registered at West Derby and in June 1867, that of Mary Prosser was registered at Liverpool. These are probably Joseph's two children referred to earlier. The 1871 Census shows Joseph William living with his mother Kate Prosser, a widow, and his sister, Mary, in St Martin in the Fields, London, with Thomas and Ellen O'Connor, sister of Kate. Kate remarried in 1873 in London, her new husband being Hugh Lunny, a Chelsea 'Out-Pensioner', i.e. not resident at the Royal Chelsea Hospital. She died in Chorlton, Lancashire, in 1905. Her third child Ellen, born in Singapore in 1860, presumably while they were abroad during Joseph's army service, is shown in the 1871 Census as being an inmate of the Royal Patriotic Asylum for Girls in London. Mary seems to have died when she was about 18 years of age. Joseph William married and went to live in Manchester; he died in 1930.

Joseph Prosser's Victoria Cross is currently on display in the Royal Scots Museum, Edinburgh Castle.

# *A*rthur Herbert Lindsay Richardson VC

A rthur Richardson was born on 23 September 1872 at 7 Leicester Street, Southport, the son of William Duke Richardson and his wife, Caroline. Records show that William Duke Richardson was a native of Annagh, County Tyrone and married Caroline, who was born in Peterborough, on 13th December 1865 in St John's Parish Church, Peterborough. Interestingly her maiden name is shown as Richardson also and there is an entry in the 1861 Census which shows a Caroline Richardson, of about the same age, living in Peterborough. His father was a general agent in insurance and was sole representative for R. Manders & Co., brewers of Dublin and also for Joshua Tetley & Sons, brewers, of Leeds. He had an office and stores in 7, York Street, 17, Henry Street, and at 50, Duke Street, Liverpool. Caroline's father and grandfather were both veterinary surgeons. Arthur was baptised at Trinity Church, Southport on 22 February 1873.

**King George V at a review in Liverpool, 19 July 1924. Arthur Richardson VC is 3rd from right wearing no medals.**

In 1881 the family lived in 'Ravensmore', Roe Lane, Southport and consisted of William, Caroline, their eight children and three servants. According to the 1881 Census, Arthur had two older sisters, two older brothers, three younger brothers and a younger sister. The four eldest were born in Eccles while the other five, including Arthur, were born in Southport. By the 1891 Census, the family had moved to live at 41 Rodney Street, Liverpool. By this time, William

**41 Rodney Street. Home of Arthur Herbert Richardson VC 1883-1894**

had died (in 1888) and Carrie (Caroline) was living with six of her children, five servants and no less than nine boarders, including cotton broker's agents and two doctors and surgeons. It seems that Arthur was educated at the Liverpool Institute. Although in all the Censuses 'Lindsay' is shown as the spelling, the family is descended from the Lords Lindesay of Byres, a noble family in the border regions of Scotland with a title dating from 1445. The surname or Christian name 'Lindesay', sometimes corrupted to 'Lindsay', has featured prominently in the Richardson family throughout the centuries and does to this day.

Arthur was apprenticed to work for a dental surgeon, Mr. R.H. Bates, of 60 Rodney Street, who was a partner in the firm of Royston & Matthews, while two of Arthur's brothers were medical agents and the other an apprentice electrical engineer. Young Arthur, however, was looking for something more adventurous and emigrated to Canada when he was about 19. After a couple of years living in Stoney Mountain, Manitoba, practising as a dentist, he went to Regina, Saskatchewan and on 7 May 1894 joined the North West Mounted Police. After his training he was posted to Battleford, at the confluence of the Battle and Saskatchewan Rivers, and settled as one of the law enforcement officers. He was promoted to corporal on 1 December 1898.

Meanwhile, Arthur's widowed mother and family lived at 'The Nook', West Albert Road, Sefton Park, Liverpool (1901 Census), but moved to 4 Mannering Road, still in Sefton Park, after that.

On 14 February 1900 he enlisted in Lord Strathcona's Horse at Chapleau, when he was 27 years old, as a corporal. He was promoted to sergeant on 10 March 1900 as the Canadian Force arrived in South Africa. The regimental Diary shows that the voyage was not a comfortable experience – entries for March 1900 describe how 'the ship [the Elder Dempster SS *Monterey*] still rolls and the horses are suffering very much, many men on board are sick'. Between 18 and 21 March, 25 horses died on board. Interestingly, on their first day at sea,

18 March 1900, 'two stowaways both of whom are deserters from the RRCI' were found.

It was not long before Arthur was in action and on 5 July 1900 at Wolvespruit, a party of Lord Strathcona's Horse, only 38 in number, was engaged by a force of 80 of the enemy. When the order to retire had been given it was noticed that Corporal Alex McArthur had been wounded twice and had had his horse shot from under him. Sergeant Richardson rode back several hundred yards under a very heavy crossfire and picked him up and rode with him out of fire. At the time Sergeant Richardson was within 300 yards of the enemy, and was himself riding a wounded horse. With the wounded man behind him, Richardson galloped back to camp, under a constant hail of fire. One bullet pierced his stetson and two others ripped his tunic. An account of Richardson's daring by another officer, Captain Agar Adamson, describes the deed:

*His horse, a small one, could only go slowly. Sergeant Buchanan and six men covered his retreat, among them George Sparks, who though shot in the neck at the time dismounted and covered the retreat. (Just when the escape seemed possible) fate intervened in the form of a wire fence which Richardson's horse, now covered with foam and thoroughly exhausted, refused to jump. The Boers closed on Richardson, demanding his surrender, when a Boer bullet struck the horse's shoulder causing it to plunge over the fence and gallop madly towards the camp and safety. The faithful animal, however, died one hour later from its wounds and the exhaustion of the chase.*

The award of the Victoria Cross was gazetted on 14 September 1900; Richardson was the first colonial and the first member of the Canadian Forces under British command to win the coveted award. In the Regimental Museum in Calgary, Alberta, is a tableau which depicts the act which earned Richardson his VC.

On 16 March 1901, Richardson was discharged in Ottawa. One document reports that whilst in Ottawa 'he borrowed money which he was rather slow in paying back'. Despite this, he rejoined the North West Mounted Police at Battleford, was promoted to sergeant on 1 July 1901 and sergeant major on 23 May 1903. He served at Battleford until 1906 although reports indicate that 'he was unable to do his job as he was sick much of the time with a variety of complaints'. On 12 November 1907 he bought his discharge from the Mounted Police, and became the 'Town Constable' of Indian Head, Saskatchewan for a short time. He claimed that he had to leave the police because of the ill health of his wife, who was unable to stand the rigours of the cold Canadian winters.

However, a town official wrote a letter on behalf of the Mayor of Indian Head to the Commissioner, North West Mounted Police at Regina, which indicates another reason for his leaving Indian Head. This letter was written on 24 February 1908, after he had ceased employment, and described him as being 'in destitute circumstances'. Richardson had been Town Constable for only four months, but the writer explained that 'the Council could not retain him in its employ and without being more specific I must say that his financial affairs were in such shape that he was always without funds. As he had to handle considerable sums for the Council, this could not be. At present, the Council is extending charity to him, his wife and child. Whilst he is under the doctor's care at the present time, he is able to do certain classes of work but there is nothing the Council can offer him which he can be trusted to do'. The writer asked whether there was any possibility of the NWMP helping Richardson but the Commissioner, whilst sympathising with Richardson's unfortunate condition, noted that it was impossible for them to help him. Subsequently, NWMP stated that Richardson 'was ruined by being awarded the Victoria Cross' as he expected everything to come his way after he had been decorated. They wrote that he had been a good constable and corporal before the award but deteriorated thereafter, 'being a victim of drink'.

In about 1901, Arthur had married Florence Elizabeth Hughes in Battleford and they had a daughter, Dorothy Alexandra Lindesay, born on 10 July 1902. Dorothy was educated at St. Margaret's Convent in Liverpool, suggesting that Florence came back to this country before Arthur. His daughter eventually held a position as a companion with a Dr. Hamilton and his family at Queen's College, Belfast. Arthur's wife died around the time he arrived back in Liverpool.

His mother had been a friend of Lady Strathcona, and this was instrumental in his gaining admission to the Mounted Police, and no doubt explains his enlistment in Strathcona's Horse. On his being awarded the Victoria Cross, Lord Strathcona sent a letter of congratulations to his mother in Liverpool. Arthur received his Cross from King Edward VII in 1902, and while in this country for the investiture chose to spend some days in Liverpool, during which time he visited Port Sunlight where he was accorded a fine welcome. He experienced other instances of impromptu celebrations in the city as word went round about who he was and of his gallant deeds. However, before this he had visited Liverpool in February 1901 when the regiment of Lord Strathcona's Horse were in England after service in South Africa and amongst other events were entertained at Buckingham Palace by King Edward VII.

The local newspapers gave extensive coverage to this visit, especially the proceedings of 23 February, when the Regiment attended a reception in

St George's Hall before embarking for Canada. During the ceremony, which saw a 'tableau of surpassing brilliancy' witnessed by a packed house, the Lord Mayor asked Sergeant Richardson, 'if he was present', to stand. Sergeant Richardson did so and 'was greeted with tumultuous cheering from all parts of the hall'. Arthur then briefly thanked those present for their ovation and announced that he had done no more than any other man in Strathcona's would have done. Interestingly, the Lord Mayor referred to Richardson as 'Liverpool born' and 'from a Liverpool family'.

In March 1924, a most amazing and bizarre picture unfolded. It came in a newspaper item from Aberdeen where an ex-Gordon Highlander had died. He was well known in the city as Corporal A. Richardson, and had been feted and acknowledged as the gallant holder of a Victoria Cross won while serving with Lord Strathcona's Horse in South Africa in 1900. For nine years since he arrived in Aberdeen he had given the impression that he was the rightful holder of the VC, so much so that when he first arrived there he made it known that he had been forced to walk the streets to find work. In spite of the difficult times, he was found a job on the railway at Cruden Bay, but was later paid off and then took a job as doorman at the Picture House where he became a well known figure and wore his crimson ribbon on his uniform. He was introduced to Earl Haig on the occasion of his visit to the city, and was given prominence at the Armistice and other parades. He even attended the Garden Party for VC heroes at Buckingham Palace, and was presented to the King.

When he died suddenly on 16 February 1924, he was buried with full military honours in Springbank Cemetery. Pallbearers were supplied from the Depot of the Gordon Highlanders and the cortege was headed by the pipe band of the British Legion with the drummers of the Gordons. The Last Post was sounded at the graveside and representatives of the British Legion, United Services Club, Gordon Highlanders Club, Freemasons, and a number of prominent citizens attended. His remains were conveyed on a gun carriage supplied by the 75th Brigade, Royal Field Artillery.

It appears that the Aberdeen Richardson came to this country from South Africa in 1915, went to Tower Hill recruiting office in London and joined the Gordon Highlanders, giving his name as Arthur Henry Leonard Richardson. He claimed to have been a private in the 2nd Durban Light Infantry and later produced a typewritten document saying that he, Arthur Henry Leonard Richardson, had won the Victoria Cross with Strathcona's Horse in the Boer War. He was promoted at once to his old rank of corporal and it seems nobody checked his story. Sent to France, he was offered a commission but refused it. He was later invalided out of the service with a disability pension for a severely wounded leg. He could give no account of his movements between leaving the Army and arriving in Aberdeen, or information about his family. He did claim to have been born in Methlick, Aberdeenshire, but no trace of his birth could be found in the records. His date of birth, 29 February 1876, makes him four years younger than the genuine Richardson, and of course the impostor used the Christian name Henry instead of Herbert.

Enquiries by journalists from the *Aberdeen Press & Journal* identified areas of discrepancy within his account and there were many instances that suggested fantasy, such as a fortune in South Africa and a claim that he had been born in India, the son of an Army Captain. My own enquiry to the Gordon Highlanders brought the kind of response that fits in with this man's story: 'We are sorry to say that we are unable to find any information whatsoever in our records of the Regiment, reference Cpl. Arthur Henry Leonard Richardson'.

On 7 April 1924 the *Liverpool Echo* had been in contact with the real Arthur Herbert Lindsay Richardson, who was now working in a tracklaying gang for the Liverpool Corporation Tramways.

Because of his straitened circumstances he had not been in touch with his family since he came to this country for his presentation. In fact, in an interview published in the *Empire News* on Sunday 6 April 1924 Arthur is quoted as saying: 'My wife is dead now so I harm nobody if I admit that my marriage did not meet with the approval of my people. I was quite a young chap when I went to Canada to join the North West Mounted Police'. This could well be the real reason why he had had no contact with his mother for some 20 years. It is difficult to understand his mother's disapproval of his marriage, except perhaps that it took place so far away and so soon after his arrival in Canada, as his wife seems to have been from a well-respected family. To leap ahead a little, his obituary, published in the *Saskatchewan Herald* of 24 December 1932, described his wife as the sister of the wife of the Hudson Bay Company's manager in Battleford.

The April 1924 interview in the *Liverpool Echo* came about because Arthur had read in the *Echo* of the death in Aberdeen of his impersonator and felt that he now had to speak out. There had been tales, believed by many, that he had died in Canada although his mother said she had always believed him to be alive. Arthur was now reunited with his mother and elder brother at their beautiful home in Mannering Road. However, he evidently had no wish to intrude on their comfortable life for he declared that he would carry on with his labouring job, and returned to his lodgings at 144 St. Domingo Vale, Everton, Liverpool. His mother died just two years later on 24 September 1926, at her home.

The more he thought about the impudence of the Aberdeen man, the less reticent he became about his life, and he often spoke of how much better things might have been if he had not been of such a quiet disposition. It was when he saw the report of 'his' death in his local paper that he decided he must come out of his shell, for people might think *he* was the imposter. Discussing his career in the North West Mounted Police he said that the members of that force had to be 'all-round' men in the most comprehensive sense of the term. They had to be able to do almost anything, especially where horses were concerned. He was paid 50 cents a day extra for breaking in horses. At the time of the great Yukon gold rush of 1894, he went to bring down the first pack of Husky dogs that carried the mails. He and others went 160 miles from Battleford to an Indian reservation where the pack of sixty dogs was waiting. They brought them along the same trail used by the prospectors who struggled to the goldfield with so much suffering, and being on horseback had a much easier journey than the gold seekers. Some dogs were driven before them, the others were attached to the patrol wagon, but they had to 'foot it' all the way. The dogs were used by the North West Mounted Police for carrying mail between Dawson City and White Pass, a journey of 240 miles, which they did once a week. While in the Mounted Police he was one of four winners of the Victoria Cross chosen in the escort at the Coronation of King Edward VII. He was an escort when the King was in Canada as Prince of Wales, and also on the occasion of the visit by Prince Arthur of Connaught.

That his secret was out did cause him some embarrassment from spectators and sightseers as he worked on the roads in Kirkdale. It is not known whether he attended any of the Garden Parties at a later date and it rather looks as if he was content to lead an unobtrusive existence, for no later references to him can be found. Enquiries made to Merseyside Transport show that his records were probably destroyed in an air-raid, and it can only be assumed that he continued in his job of tracklaying. He drew his VC pension each year without difficulty but always asked the police to sign his papers as confirmation. It seems likely that the Aberdeen Richardson could not have drawn a pension and it was puzzling to Arthur that the impostor had been invited to the Palace without somebody questioning his address.

Arthur died in Mill Road Hospital on 15 December 1932, aged 59 years, and was buried in St. James's Cemetery (No. 57679). The burial service was conducted by the Reverend Canon Henry Walker Campbell Baugh MA, the Vicar of St. Brides Church, Catherine Street. An account in the *Liverpool Echo* of Monday 7 April 1924 stated:

*The romance of Liverpool's long-hidden V.C., Sergeant A.H.L.*
*Richardson, Strathcona's Horse, who has for years worked as a*

*tramway ganger while an impostor enjoyed the honours rightfully belonging to Richardson, reached a happy climax yesterday, when the son 'who was dead and is alive again' was reunited with his mother and elder brother at their home in Mannering Road, Sefton Park.*

*This was their first meeting for over twenty years. For the last nine years Sergeant Richardson had been believed to be dead, a message to that effect having been sent to his mother by a nurse in a Montreal hospital. As fully recounted by the Echo, the V.C. had been working as a labourer, cinema attendant, and so forth in Liverpool for over sixteen years, unknown to his relatives, the reason being that his straitened circumstances disinclined him to reveal himself. Richardson told our representative the story of his reunion with his mother and brother last evening, refuting at the outset a report that he was 'trembling' when he called at the house. 'I'm not the man to tremble at anything', he said, laughing at the idea.*

*'I rang the bell, one of the maids answered. I asked if Mrs. Richardson was in, and the maid said she was resting. I believe she took me to be another reporter! Then I asked if Mr. Robert Richardson (Arthur's older brother) was in, and she replied that he too was resting. Could I come back in an hour? I said I thought I could, and she asked was it anything important, and I said no, not particularly, only I'm a Mr. Richardson myself. With that she fled, leaving the door open, and rushed upstairs to tell my mother. My brother came down first, and he was delighted to see me. He shook me warmly by the hand and then my mother came down. The joy on her face was enough to repay me for a very great deal.*

*During the evening I met also my niece, who like my daughter in Ireland, is named Dorothy, and is about 22 years of age. My girl was educated at St. Margaret's Convent, Liverpool, and I haven't seen her since she went to Ireland eleven years ago to act, I believe, as a companion in Dr. Hamilton's family at Queen's College, Belfast. When my niece came to me and said she was Dorothy, I thought for a moment it was my own daughter'.*

*'Well everything's all right again now', said the V.C. with a contented sigh, 'but I intend to carry on my work as a labourer until something else turns up. I don't know of any probable change in that direction, but I suppose it is quite possible that I may find something better. In the meantime I'm taking a little rest. I have become too well known to*

*the public now to feel like going back in the particular road where I have been working during the last week. Crowds came to look at me, and even passengers on tramcars pointed me out to one another'.*

He also found that he was receiving congratulatory mail and, it being a leap year, there were quite a number of 'interesting enquiries' from the opposite sex. The *Echo* published the contents of two of them. Arthur made a point of declaring that he was a freemason, an Oddfellow, and a Forester, belonging to Canadian lodges. (He certainly did not make use of their services to improve his circumstances.).

Someone calling himself Arthur H.L. Richardson VC attended a garden party hosted by King George V on 26 June 1920, but this was almost certainly the imposter. The true Richardson was present on Saturday 19 July 1924 when the King reviewed the 55th West Lancashire Territorial Division at Wavertree Playground, Liverpool. Arthur was one of nine holders of the Victoria Cross presented to His Majesty. Others included Cyril Gourley VC, William Heaton VC, Arthur Procter VC, Ronald Stuart VC, John Molyneux VC and John Davies VC, all of whom feature or will feature in this series of books. A photograph taken that day shows Arthur Richardson with three other VC holders being inspected by the King. Interestingly, Arthur is wearing no medals - a reflection on the hard times which caused him to pawn them in Canada. He obviously did not redeem them. In this context, there is a report stating that Arthur received £3000 collected by the people of Canada for their first VC. It is not clear whether this was a 'spur of the moment' gesture, although a report in the *Liverpool Daily Post* on 23 February 1901 seems to indicate that this was a 'prize' collected in advance in the event that a Canadian might win the Victoria Cross. Whichever is true, there can be no doubt that it did not last very long in Arthur's hands, despite the fact that in today's terms this would be somewhere in the region of £300,000! [We would be interested in identifying the other

**Headstone to AHL Richardson VC, close to Liverpool Cathedral (Anglican)**

three VC winners in the photograph on p.85 although the uniformed officer is almost certainly Cyril Gourley.]

For many years the exact location of Arthur's grave in St James's Cemetery has been unknown but there is now a Commonwealth War Graves Commission-style headstone, erected in 1996, just inside the main gate to the precincts of Liverpool's Anglican Cathedral. It is sited close to the former cemetery, and almost directly opposite Rodney Street, where Arthur Richardson lived. Sid Lindsay played a major part in causing this headstone to be erected. It is easily missed but in recent years a poppy wreath has been laid at its foot. In November 2006 it was laid by cadets of the Irish Guards Battalion from Crosby during a sponsored walk which they and others undertook, visiting the graves of all the Victoria Cross holders who are buried in the Liverpool area. Arthur Richardson's Victoria Cross is displayed in the Canadian War Museum, Montreal, Canada.

## *Postscript*

Early in 2007, Mr Alexander Low and his son visited Liverpool to find Richardson's grave. They are descendants of Arthur through his sister, Mabel Emily. They found the headstone in the grounds of the Cathedral, noted the poppy wreath which had been laid and made enquiries as to who might have laid it. Fortunately they spoke to David Hudson, a member of the NCVCMA committee and a guide at the Cathedral. David put me in touch with the visitors, as a result of which a great deal of the information in this chapter was passed to me. I am grateful to Mr Low, particularly for the photographs to which he allowed me access. He had recently visited the Strathconas' Museum in Calgary and personally took photographs of the tableau. It was he who provided me with the photograph with King George V and an enthralling copy of their family tree, filled with details of interesting ancestors, such as Alexander Lindsay who was killed on the walls of Derry during the 17th century siege; or Walter Richardson, of the 9th Regiment of Foot and Captain of the Dungannon Militia in the 18th century. He also brought to my attention the fact that Arthur's daughter, Dorothy, at least until 1984, was living at 297 Queens Drive, Stoneycroft, Liverpool. If she were still alive (and I have not yet resolved her date of death), she would now be 104 years old.

*Bill Sergeant*

# *J*ohn Alexander Sinton
## VC

**John Alexander Sinton VC**

orn on 2 December 1884 in Victoria, British Columbia, Canada, John Alexander Sinton was the son of Walter Lyon Sinton, and of Isabella (née Pringle). His father was the eldest son of John Sinton, the manager of the Ravaruette Linen Mill, Co. Down, Northern Ireland, and his mother was the daughter of Alexander Pringle, manager of the linen mill at Bessbrook, in Co. Armagh. Walter Sinton emigrated to the United States of America, moved on to Canada, and after a number of years returned to the United States. He was a writer and travelled extensively on the North American continent.

John Sinton was educated at the Nicholson Memorial School, later at the Royal Belfast Academical Institution, and Queen's College, Belfast. From here he went to Queen's University, Belfast and in 1908 graduated with first class honours in Medicine, taking degrees of Bachelor of Medicine, Bachelor in Surgery, and Bachelor in Art of Obstetrics. He became Riddell Demonstrator in the pathology department of Queen's, and held an appointment in pathology at the Liverpool School of Tropical Medicine. After house appointments, he took a Diploma in Public Health at Belfast and Cambridge, followed by a Diploma in Tropical Medicine at Liverpool. In 1911, he entered the Indian Medical Service, gaining first place in the entrance examination. Previously, he had spent a short time as the Medical Officer to the 31st Bengal Lancers, where he was extremely popular with all ranks and their families.

At the outbreak of the First World War, Sinton was on active service on the volatile and dangerous North West Frontier of India. He was soon to join the newly assembled Mesopotamian Expeditionary Force, taking part in the campaign in this 'land that God forgot'. His short experience in tropical medicine came to the fore, as there were more casualties from disease and pestilence than from the horrors perpetrated by the Turks and rebel Arabs. As a medical officer with the Indian Cavalry he was destined to be always close to the front line action when the cavalry led advances across the wastelands of the Euphrates and Tigris. On 21 January 1916 Captain John Sinton earned his Victoria Cross in action at Sheik Sa'ed in the area of the Orah Ruins, one of the attempts made to relieve the siege at Kut-el-Amara. His citation read, in part:

> *For most conspicuous bravery and devotion to duty. Although shot through both arms and through the side he refused to go to hospital, and remained as long as the daylight lasted, attending to his duties under very heavy fire. In three previous actions Captain Sinton had displayed the utmost bravery.*

Those few lines from his citation inadequately describe the circumstances that prevailed for the troops of the Expeditionary Force, where the terrain of ridges and scrubland provided the enemy with so many defensive advantages, and where the British lack of local knowledge hampered deployment. All too often the ground was swept from different directions with artillery, rifle and machine gun fire from snipers hidden in the dried-up gulleys. In addition there was the heat and dust to be contended with - to rescue and attend to the wounded in the open and in daylight was little short of suicidal.

John Sinton was eventually invalided back to India, but he was soon back in action on the North West Frontier. In 1917, the Irish Medical Schools and Graduates Association awarded him the Arnott Memorial Medal. By the end of the Great War he had been Mentioned in Dispatches four times, and had also received the Russian Order of St. George. The Captain was presented with his Victoria Cross on 31 January 1918 by Lord Chelmsford, the Viceroy of India, at a ceremony in Delhi.

He was promoted Brevet Major in 1919, and Queen's University conferred the honorary degree of Doctor of Medicine upon him 'in recognition of his early distinctions and of his valour in the field while engaged in the treatment and succour of the wounded'. He saw further service on the north-west frontier in Afghanistan and Waziristan, being Mentioned in Dispatches on two occasions, and for his services he was awarded the Order of the British Empire in 1921. He then retired from the Army, having spent ten years on truly active service.

His return to civilian life saw him begin his career in medical research in earnest when he entered the Medical Research Department of the Indian Medical Service to take charge of a special inquiry into the treatment of malaria. He was involved in the setting up of a malaria treatment centre at Kasauli, in the Punjab, and the experiments carried out there under his direction brought a rational approach to the treatment and development of anti-malarial drugs towards the prevention of relapse of the disease. His meticulous and diligent attention to the problems resulted in the occurrence of relapsing malaria being reduced to negligible figures in the Army in India. He had gathered around him a team of outstanding research workers who were readily inspired by his dedication and concern, and he came to be recognised as a foremost authority on malarial and parasitical diseases. On 24 March 1927 he was awarded the degree of Doctor of Science, and in the same year was appointed the first Director of the Malarial Survey of India. He founded a scientific journal to publish updated information on the treatment of the disease and the subsequent control of the breeding areas of the mosquito. He also published some 200 papers on entomology that added much to the world's knowledge of parasitical infections.

In 1928, Sinton was awarded the Chalmers Memorial Medal of the Royal Society of Tropical Medicine and Hygiene. He continued to pursue his endeavours in the prevention of disease until 1938, when he retired from the Indian Medical Service. He was then appointed Manson Fellow of the London School of Hygiene and Tropical Medicine, and advisor on malaria to the Ministry of Health. On the outbreak of war in 1939, he was recalled to India and posted as Quartermaster to a military hospital where he was to prove an outstanding success. The following year he was demobilised on reaching the age of 55, but almost immediately was recalled to be appointed as Consultant Malariologist to the East African Forces, and this was later extended to cover the whole of the Middle East Forces (MEF). He applied himself as always in the most conscientious way, fully realising the dangers of malarial exposure to the masses of troops newly arriving from the United Kingdom and the Empire. As the need for specialised medical supplies required considerable organisation to ensure that they were readily available, he directed the careful advanced planning to this end, and largely through his expertise the incidence of malaria in the MEF was minimal. Having established a logical procedure for prevention and control, he was retired yet again in 1944, only to be recalled and appointed as Consultant Malariologist to the War Office as a result of many serious outbreaks of the disease as troops moved into Sicily and Italy.

The end of the war also brought about his final retirement. He had been awarded the Blisset-Hawkins Medal by the Royal College of Physicians, in London, and in 1946 became the Robert Campbell Memorial Orator and Medallist of the Ulster Medical Society. He had retired with the rank of Brigadier, and settled at Slaghtfreedan Lodge, Cookstown, Co. Tyrone Northern Ireland, to enjoy the life of a country gentleman, indulging in ornithology, fishing and gardening, all a far cry from the world of medical science and the rigours of war. In 1949, he was awarded the coveted Mary Kingsley Medal by the Liverpool School of Tropical Medicine. [The Mary Kingsley Medal was established in 1905, in commemoration of the work of Mary Kingsley in West Africa. She travelled widely in Africa in the 1890s and became a figure of national importance due to her intrepid research into primitive religious beliefs. She later went to South Africa, and there died nursing Boer prisoners. The Medal in her honour is presented by the School to individuals who have made notable contributions to the study of tropical medicine. John Sinton received his medal along with others on the occasion of the fiftieth anniversary of the School's opening. The School is affiliated to the University of Liverpool.]

John Sinton married, in 1923, Eadith Seymour Steuart Martin, the only daughter of the late Edward Steuart Martin, of Azamgarh, Uttar Pradesh, India, who had been an indigo planter. They had a daughter, Eleanor, who married Dr. Hubert Watson and spent many years in medical research in West Africa before retiring to a well-earned rest in Ireland.

Although John Sinton had left his medical and Army interests behind, preferring the quiet life in Ireland, he participated in local affairs. He became a Justice of the Peace, was a Deputy Lieutenant, and in 1953 was High Sheriff for Tyrone and served on the National Arbitration Tribunal of Northern Ireland. He also became President of the Cookstown Branch of the British Legion, taking a prominent interest in the affairs of the Branch, always showing concern for his fellow comrades-in-arms.

On 25 March 1956 John Sinton died at the age of 72 years, having known for eight years that he was terminally ill, appreciating better than most the implications of his failing health, yet he never allowed it to make any difference to his work or social life, continuing to give support and help to many voluntary bodies particularly those connected with ex-servicemen. His funeral took place on 28 March at the Claggan Presbyterian Churchyard where the service was conducted at the graveside, following a service at his home. The coffin, on which rested the Brigadier's dress sword, his cap and medals, was draped with the Union Flag and carried into the cemetery by the vice-presidents of the Cookstown British Legion along with the Branch's Standard which was escorted by the Branch Chairman, and another local official. The procession was preceded by two pipers from the Depot of the Royal Inniskilling Fusiliers at Omagh, who played the lament. At the graveside the Final Salute was fired by two NCOs and 12 Fusiliers, while *Reveille* and the *Last Post* were sounded by a bugler from the Depot. The local members of the British Legion filed past the grave, each dropping a poppy onto the coffin. The ceremony was attended by leading members of the British Legion, the medical profession, Queen's University, and many other prominent figures representing the range of John Sinton's interests to the community at large.

There is a moving ceremony which to this day takes place each year at the grave of Brigadier Sinton VC, at the Claggan Cemetery, when the Cookstown Branch of the Royal British Legion lay a poppy wreath, on the Saturday afternoon before Remembrance Sunday.

The Royal British Legion Housing Association (N.I.) Ltd., in 1987 completed a small housing complex of seven single storey houses - two semi-detached blocks, and a block of three, which are now occupied by seven elderly ex-service couples. It was officially opened by John Sinton's daughter, Mrs Eleanor Watson, and has been named Sinton Court, in his honour and memory.

John Sinton had always maintained a close and active interest in Queen's University, Belfast, and his services were appropriately recognised when he was appointed Pro-Chancellor in 1952, a position he held until his death in 1956. In his memory one of the Halls of Residence has been named Sinton Hall.

Brigadier John Sinton was recalled by his contemporaries as a man with an exceptionally quick intellect and a flair for getting to the heart of any problem. He was a man of the highest integrity and of great moral and physical courage. He always did what he felt to be right no matter how unpopular his actions might prove to be; he loathed expediency. These characteristics and his uncompromising attitude sometimes brought him into conflict with higher authority, and this may explain the paucity of official recognition of the great work that he did. No one could have been kinder, or more understanding and considerate to his older and younger colleagues, and all who worked with him had the greatest respect and affection for him.

He was seen as a tall, spare man, active and full of energy, who threw himself into whatever work he had in hand, and did not waiver until it was completed. He was forthright and outspoken, and did not suffer fools gladly. The kindest and most generous of souls, whose gospel in life was to give ungrudgingly of his best, a loyal friend.

39 men of the Army Medical Services have earned the Victoria Cross since its inception, and of the three men who have earned a Bar to their Victoria Cross, two of them were in the medical profession. John Alexander Sinton was another hero in every sense of the word, of whom the Army Medical Services can justly be proud. He is the only Fellow of the Royal Society to have been awarded the Victoria Cross, which is displayed in the Army Medical Service Museum, Aldershot.

**Grave of JA Sinton VC at Claggan Churchyard (Presbyterian)**

# AMENDMENTS TO *LIVERPOOL HEROES* BOOK I

It was inevitable that following the publication of Book 1, additional information would be forthcoming from interested readers. I am most grateful for readers' input, and would ask that any corrections or additions to information about the 'Heroes' in Book 2 be sent to me via the address given at the front of the book.

I am now able to make the following amendments to Book 1:

## Gabriel George Coury VC

Coury's great-grandson, Steve Shepherd, makes the following comments:

'I don't believe that Raphael's father was Basil Coury – I think Basil was probably a brother or cousin. In the 1881 Census, Basil is described as a 32-year-old clerk from Egypt, sharing lodgings with a Syrian and neither was married. Raphael was born in 1859 so Basil was only about 10 years older than him. Also in 1881, a Basil Coury appears in a Census in British Egypt on the Comores Islands – no wife there either. (Possibly the same persons in both Censuses?) We have a set of cousins who were born in Alexandria but we are unsure who was their grandfather – it is my guess, and a pure guess, that it might have been Basil.

Marie's naturalisation papers say that Raphael was born in Beyrut (Beirut) in modern day Lebanon but then in Syria. Both Syria and Egypt were under the control of the Ottoman Empire (Turkey) and the 'smart' language spoken by the upper classes within the Ottoman Empire was French so I suspect Raphael was also a Francophone.

Some references suggest that the family were Armenians – I can find no evidence of that. My aunt, now deceased, used to say that the family came from Aleppo, which would be feasible as Aleppo has always been one of the principal trading cities in the history of the region. Every branch of the family has always been Catholic; as Book I states, Gabriel and Maurice were educated at Stonyhurst College while Charles was educated at Mount St Mary's College in Eckington – another Jesuit independent school. The cousins in Alexandria are all Catholics as well. Charles died on 15 December 1970 and not as stated; his wife, Winifred, died in Southport 6 years later. Maurice died on 17 April 1928 when he was 30.

The section that says Coury went to Egypt between the wars is incorrect, as is the reference to his wife running the chip-shop in his absence! Gabriel separated from his wife before the Second World War and she died in August 1976. As devout Catholics, there was no possibility of them getting a divorce. The lady in the chip-shop was not his wife but a partner in the business. The last of Raphael's children, Louise Andre, died in the 1990s and is buried in Roehampton. Charles died in Sidmouth'.

## Alfred Stowell Jones VC

His eldest son and Captain of the *Africa* was Harry Jones. The son killed in India in 1895 was Martin, born in 1873. Percy was the son killed at Samara in 1917.

## William Ratcliffe VC

Mrs Noreen Hill has kindly supplied the following correct information: she was the daughter of Margaret Walsh (nee Humes) and grand-daughter of Sarah Humes (née Ratcliffe). Sarah's husband, John, did not always see eye to eye with his brother-in-law Bill although he did live with them and his other sister from time to time. When John Humes died in 1948, Bill went to live with his sister Sarah at 30 Head Street, Liverpool and moved with her to 29a St Oswald Gardens, Old Swan. Sarah died in 1955 and Bill remained at St Oswald's Gardens until his death in 1963. He is buried with his sister Sarah and her husband John Humes in Allerton Cemetery.

# APPENDIX I

## The Memorial

The Memorial to Noel Chavasse, VC and Bar, an adopted son of Liverpool, and 15 other recipients of the Victoria Cross who were born in Liverpool, is the brainchild of local Chavasse admirers. They met in July 2005 and declared their intention of securing a fitting memorial. Ambitious? Optimistic? Foolhardy? My answer to each would have to be 'Yes!' – but the group's determination to succeed has never wavered.

The sculptor is a local man, Tom Murphy, who has a long history of producing memorable pieces in Liverpool. He is responsible for the Shankly statue at Liverpool Football Club, the John Lennon statue at our airport, the Moores Brothers statue formerly in Church Street but now in Old Hall Street, the Captain Johnny Walker statue at the Pier Head, the Blitz Memorial at Liverpool Parish Church, and many others.

It seemed logical to us that Tom should be our man, especially as we knew he shared our admiration for Chavasse and our other 'Liverpool Heroes'. We consulted the Chavasse family and the Regimental Associations and all agreed that we should aim for a traditional bronze work which would strive to show the character and personality of Noel Chavasse, rather than a particular moment in history.

We also agreed that both the Royal Army Medical Corps and the Liverpool Scottish allegiances of Chavasse should feature, together with one of his stretcher-bearers - Noel was always anxious to remind people of their bravery. Within these parameters, Tom's design has found favour not only with us but also with the family and military, and I leave it to him to describe our memorial.

**Bill Sergeant, Chairman, NCVCMA**

## Design of the NCVCMA Memorial

It was decided almost from the outset that the Chavasse sculpture celebrating the heroic deeds of Captain Noel Chavasse could not be depicted using a single figure. He was not a glory seeker; his deeds arose from his dedication as a doctor, a real professional and above all a committed Christian. He would not have been comfortable with a statue which did not pay tribute to a brave stretcher-bearer. A wounded soldier became the third figure.

A three-figure grouping provided an ideal opportunity for an action sculpture, and a work which is meant to be interesting from all viewing angles. The sculptural group forms an offset triangle, or a wave set on a slight gradient. The angular lines throughout the piece create an impression of forward propulsion and a sense of struggle. In line with the conditions of the time, the figures look as if they are on an endless challenging journey.

The figures are displayed on an oblong base reminiscent of the Cenotaph, and the sloped sides of the base include tributes to 15 Liverpool-born Victoria Cross winners. Captain Chavasse is portrayed straining under the weight of the wounded soldier, whose whole body and arms are extended across the length of the sculpture in a cruciform shape.

The sculpture has many fine details: Chavasse himself is depicted wearing the Liverpool Scottish Glengarry with his RAMC uniform – perhaps not strictly accurate in the context of battle but symbolic of his everlasting affection for the Liverpool Battalion. He supports a wounded soldier by stretching his right arm over his shoulder and clasping the wrist of the wounded man. At the same time, he supports the wounded man's upper torso with his other arm.

The powerful stretcher-bearer at the rear contorts his body to assist in the lift, and his concern for the wounded man's obvious ankle injury is apparent. In this kneeling position, the famous Liverpool Scottish kilt is clearly displayed. The close contact of the figures, which almost seem to be welded together, echoes the compassion and camaraderie of soldiers.

The design sets out to maintain the viewer's interest throughout with the dramatic positions of the figures set at differing heights, and the mass of detail, including the way the hands are depicted - some coupled together and others stretched out dramatically - and the detail of the badges and uniforms of the RAMC, the King's Liverpool Regiment and the Liverpool Scottish.

I have deliberately omitted any reference to the weapons of war as this sculpture is primarily about the triumph of love and compassion in laying down one's life for another. This message will be as relevant for generations to come as it was in 1914-18. It is important to emphasise that although this memorial depicts Noel Chavasse, it nevertheless commemorates the valour and deeds of fifteen other recipients of the Victoria Cross, several of whom, like Chavasse, lost their lives whilst helping their fellow men. Chavasse epitomises the bravery of all such men to whom this memorial is a lasting tribute.

I am proud to have been chosen for this Commission. My words do it scant justice for, after all, this sculpture is meant to be seen.

**Tom Murphy, Sculptor**

# APPENDIX II

## Sid Lindsay's Introduction to Book I, and his notes on the Victoria Cross

[Sid Lindsay was a local Victoria Cross enthusiast and historian, whose work on local Victoria Cross heroes has inspired the production of this series of books. Sadly, Sid passed away without knowing that his findings, augmented by later research, were to be published, but he would have been delighted to know that his 'Heroes' were to be remembered in this way. **Bill Sergeant**]

This collection of notes came about as a result of some private research I did into the businesses and trades of Merseyside. Whilst thus engaged, in 1986 I came across the name of Captain Gabriel George Coury VC, who with his family was involved in the Liverpool Cotton Trade. It then occurred to me that there was no record of local recipients of the Victoria Cross in one collection, and I decided to attempt to rectify this omission.

I naively believed that the lives of such heroes would be well-documented and that all I would need to do was to draw up a list of names and quickly gather

**Sid Lindsay at George Nurse VC's grave, Allerton, Liverpool**

together the stories of their deeds and lives. I began with an initial list of 20 names but this number soon rose to 62, some admittedly having only a slight connection with Merseyside. I had not anticipated that for many of these heroes there was little on record other than birth, death and citation. To my disappointment I quickly found that the most likely sources, such as Regimental Associations and Museums and the Royal British Legion were not the best informed and in some instances, sadly, seemed to be uninterested. As a mere novice in such matters, this lack of response caused me considerable frustration and meant that the project took much longer than I had anticipated.

I am not a military historian, nor am I a proficient storyteller. Consequently, this is simply meant to be a collection of biographical notes about some very special people. Inevitably, there will be mistakes due to my lack of expertise. I have made many errors while researching, but each has served only to make me seek another direction to find out what I needed to know. Compared to the depth of research which goes into the writing of some of the major tomes to which I have had access, my task has been of a comparatively short duration. Nevertheless it has tested my patience, as well as that of my longsuffering wife, Betty, to the limits. It has made me realise, above all, how important it is that similar exercises are undertaken to ensure that other aspects of our local history are recorded for posterity. I urge anybody who can do so to make their contribution by jotting down notes on their own lives, their family history, the firm for which they work or worked, military and public service or just memories of things that used to be. Otherwise, as with my gallant subjects, this information will be lost. Believe me, the satisfaction to be gained is considerable.

My enquiries have brought me into contact with many correspondents who share my interest in the lives of these heroic figures, awarded the nation's highest accolade for conspicuous bravery. I am truly indebted to these kind and considerate people who took the time and trouble to write to me offering valuable help and words of encouragement. I have to confess that not until this late stage of my life have I had any real knowledge of these brave men and their deeds. Like many of my contemporaries, I took such valour for granted. However, if this belated attempt at paying homage helps ensure a continuing interest in the lives of the recipients, or arouses or revives interest in other seemingly forgotten heroes, then my work will have been worthwhile.

There has been a temptation from time to time to compare one Victoria Cross deed with another, a temptation which I have tried to resist. In my somewhat elementary researches, I have been generally and genuinely appalled by the horrors which have been perpetrated and endured in the service of one's country. I am also conscious that the holders of the Victoria Cross are the selected representatives of many, many more very brave men and women who gave their all in their country's cause. I have no wish to demean the achievements of those who hold the Cross, but I feel certain that our heroes would never want us to forget their many colleagues who deserved to be recognised as much as or even more than they themselves, had fate or circumstance so decreed. My own active service was of little consequence – I was called up early in 1945 and spent most of my time in Italy, serving with the Royal Electrical and Mechanical Engineers until 1948.

Reading the numerous accounts of these great men, I constantly felt personally involved in the events that surrounded them: the great sacrifices made, the sweethearts, wives, children and parents whose pride was so severely tempered by poignant loss. I was also struck by the many mysteries with which some of our heroes surrounded themselves almost like a shield against the 'fame' attracted by their achievements. How sad it was that so many of them were eventually to leave this world friendless and almost forgotten.

I hope that these notes will be read with interest. I hope that my list is complete, but would not be surprised to learn that there are more Liverpool-born heroes than the 14 I have identified. We have good cause to be grateful to every one of them, for it is to them and their companions that we owe the quality of life which we presently enjoy.

# The Victoria Cross

Instituted on 29 January 1856, the Victoria Cross is awarded only to those of the armed forces who merit the honour – 'For Conspicuous Bravery'. The principle has been upheld that no other circumstances, neither rank, nor length of service nor severity of wounds would be considered. Initially it was awarded retrospectively to cover the Crimean War (1854-1856) and the first 62 Victoria Crosses were presented by HM Queen Victoria in Hyde Park, London on 26 June 1857.

The Cross is described as a 'cross patée of bronze, one and a half inches in diameter', and is made from the metal of Russian guns captured at Sevastopol. In the centre is the Royal Crown surmounted by a lion and beneath is a scroll with the words 'For Valour' inscribed. The date of the act of gallantry is engraved on the reverse side and the holder's name is to be found on the reverse of the clasp. The ribbon was originally blue for the Royal Navy and red for the Army, but under a Royal Warrant of 1920 this was changed to crimson for both services.

The Victoria Cross has precedence and is worn before all other decorations and on the left breast. If the ribbon only is worn, a small replica of the Cross is fixed in the centre. The award is not given lightly for there is strict scrutiny of every recommendation. A comparison seems to show that the Cross may have been awarded more frequently before the 1914-18 War than since the end of that war – for instance, the number of Victoria Crosses awarded in the Indian Mutiny was the same as for the whole of the Second World War. It must be remembered, however, that at that time the only other award available to recognise bravery in service was the Distinguished Conduct Medal, whereas now there are ten alternative honours. It would seem that a most important criterion for the Victoria Cross is that of self-sacrifice – an act of heroism, often performed on more than one occasion, in which the individual, regardless of his own safety, attempts to rescue, protect or support his fellow men or vital equipment in the face of the enemy. It also includes acts of daring leadership to secure objectives in the face of tremendous danger and in doing so to save lives and restore faltering morale. This booklet gives examples of both.

The total number of Victoria Crosses awarded up to now stands at 1355, including one to the American Unknown Soldier. 112 were awarded in the Crimean War; 182 in the Indian Mutiny; 225 for the China Campaign, Zulu War, Sudan and South African Wars. In the Great War (1914-1920), 633 were awarded; in the inter-war years, 5; and in the Second World War, 182. Since then 4 were awarded in Korea, 1 in Sarawak, 4 to Australians in Vietnam, 2 in the Falklands Conflict of 1982 and one in Iraq.

Only three people have earned double VCs; three have been awarded to fathers and sons; and four pairs of brothers have earned the award. The youngest winners – Thomas Flynn in the Indian Mutiny and Andrew Fitzgibbon in the China War of 1860 – were both just 15 years old. The oldest recipient is believed to be William Raynor during the Indian Mutiny, who was nearly 62 years of age. Accepting that the Victoria Cross is awarded only during times of conflict, it is not surprising that there are now very few surviving holders of the award. In 1952, there were 412 surviving holders; by 1976 that number had fallen to 117; and in 1984 there were only 68, of whom only 8 remained from the 1914-18 war. There are now only 12 survivors – none from the First World War – including the most recent, Private Johnson Beharry. 8 survive from the Second World War, including Liverpool's Lt Commander Ian Fraser. The last surviving Great War recipient was Air Commodore Ferdinand M.F.West who earned his VC on 10 August 1918 in France, serving with 8 Squadron Royal Air Force and died almost 80 years later in 1998. The two Falklands War recipients, Colonel H.Jones and Sergeant I.J.McKay, received their awards posthumously.

Holders of the Victoria Cross below the rank of commissioned officer were granted pensions, initially of £10 per year with £5 for a Bar. Paltry as this sum may seem, it was to remain unchanged until 1959 when the sum was increased to £100 per year, tax free, and all ranks became eligible. In 1995, the annual pension was increased to £1300. Interestingly, in a *Daily Mirror* report on 31 January 2006 about surviving VC holders, it was noted that Tulbahadur Pun VC, a Gurkha living in Nepal, was obliged to sell his VC because of financial hardship, whilst Bhanbhagta Gurung, another Gurkha also living in Nepal, found that his £1300 annual pension made him 'one of the richest men in the region'.

In the original Royal Warrant there was an expulsion clause which would permit a recipient's name to be erased from the Register for certain discreditable conduct and thereby cancel the pension. HM King George V felt strongly that there should never be any circumstances which should make the award forfeit and although the expulsion clause still remains it is highly unlikely ever to be invoked.

In 1902, King Edward VII approved the important principle of awarding the Victoria Cross posthumously; and in 1911, King George V decreed the eligibility of native officers and men of the Indian Army. In 1920, the award was extended to include the Royal Air Force and 'matrons, sisters and nurses, serving regularly or temporarily under orders, direction or supervision of the military authorities'. The decoration has never, as yet, been awarded to a woman.

One important aspect of the award is contained in what is referred to as 'Rule 13' of the Royal Warrant of 29 January 1856:

> *It is ordained that, in the event of a gallant and daring act having been performed by a squadron, ship's company, a detached body of Seamen and Marines not under 50 in number, or by a brigade, regiment company or troop, in which the Admiral, General or other Officer Commanding such forces may deem that all are equally brave and distinguished so that no special selection can be made by them, then in such case the Admiral, General or Officer Commanding may direct that for any such body of Seamen or Marines, or for every troop or company of Soldiers, that one Officer shall be selected by the Officers engaged for the decoration. And in a like manner one Petty Officer or Non-commissioned Officer shall be*

*selected by the Petty Officers and Non-commissioned Officers engaged and two Seamen or Private Soldiers or Marines shall be selected by the Seamen, Private Soldiers or Marines engaged respectively, for the decoration; and the names of those selected shall be transmitted by the Senior Officer in command of the Naval Force, Brigade, Regiment, Company or Troop, to the Admiral or General Officer Commanding who shall in due manner confer the decoration as if the acts were done under his own eye.*

That paragraph takes some reading but has affected the award to a number of recipients over the years (see for example Ronald Neil Stuart VC in *Liverpool Heroes Book I.*).

In January 2006, the VC holders still surviving were:

**Eric Wilson**, East Surrey Regiment, August 1940 in Somaliland. Now 93 years of age.

**Tulbahadur Pun**, 6th Gurkha Rifles, June 1944 in Burma. Now 82 years of age.

**John Cruickshank**, Royal Air Force Volunteer Reserve, July 1944 over the Atlantic. Now 85 years of age.

**Tasker Watkins**, The Welsh Regiment, August 1944 in Normandy. Now 87 years of age.

**Bhanbhagta Gurung**, 2nd Gurkha Rifles, March 1945 in Burma. Now 85 years of age.

**Lachhiman Gurung**, 8th Gurkha Rifles, May 1945 in Burma. Now 87 years of age.

**Ted Kenna**, Australian Imperial Force, May 1945 in New Guinea. Now aged 86 years.

**Ian Fraser**, Royal Naval Reserve, May 1945 in Singapore Harbour. Now 85 years of age.

**Bill Speakman**, Black Watch, November 1951 in Korea. Now 77 years of age.

**Rambahadur Limbu**, 2nd Battalion, 10th Princess Mary's Own Gurkha Rifles, November 1965 in Borneo. Now 66 years old.

**Keith Payne**, 1st Battalion Royal Australian Regiment, May 1969, in Vietnam. Now 72 years old.

**Johnson Beharry**, Princess of Wales's Royal Regiment, May 2004 in Iraq. Now 26 years old.

# APPENDIX III

## NCVCMA Pilgrimage to Belgium

**NCVCMA Committee members at the grave of Noel Chavasse**

Our passionate interest in the project to provide a memorial statue to our Liverpool Heroes arose from several trips we have made to the Western Front over the past five or six years. We make this pilgrimage annually and on each occasion manage to introduce new travellers to the wonders of this aspect of the Great War. When we travel to Flanders, we make a point of visiting the grave of Noel Chavasse to lay a wreath. 2007 was no exception and we have just returned from a four-day trip which was possibly the most memorable we have so far experienced.

On Friday 4 May, 43 of us, including most of our committee members together with members of the Hale and Halton Branches of the Royal British Legion, set off by coach for Calais and on to Belgium. We travelled in convoy with members of the 'Clan Wallace Pipe Band'. The Band, after a two or three years wait, had been given the privilege of leading the parade on Saturday 5 May to the Menin Gate in Ypres. We were privileged to march behind the band and take part in a moving ceremony which had all the more impact on everybody present because of the attendance of the Band.

**Chavasse's headstone**

The Deputy Lord Mayor of Hale, David Hudson, together with many others, including dignitaries, relatives, children and even members of the Gurkha Regiment, laid wreaths at this impressive British Memorial to the Missing of the Ypres Salient. It carries 54,338 names of those who died between 1914 and 15 August 1917, and who have no known grave. In particular we laid a wreath as the NCVCMA, the centrepiece to the wreath, made by Linda Darnell from our Committee, depicting Noel Chavasse, whose brother Aidan's name is on the Gate, with many other members of the King's (Liverpool) Regiment who made the ultimate sacrifice. After the ceremony our wreath was admired by many pilgrims from all over Europe. Those of you who have witnessed this daily ceremony will understand what I mean when I say that the Menin Gate experience cannot fail to strengthen our sense of gratitude to those who gave their lives. In our case, it also strengthened our determination to bring our memorial project to fruition.

Before and after our evening in Ypres, we visited many sites of daring deeds and self-sacrifice which earned many of our Liverpool Heroes their Victoria Crosses. Near the village of Passchendaele is the Tyne Cot Memorial to the Missing, which bears the names of 34,857 soldiers who died between 16 August 1917 and the end of the War; here we held a short ceremony at which a piper from the Clan Wallace Band played a lament and we laid wreaths, watched by several hundred other visitors. Tyne Cot, the largest British war cemetery in the world, is the last resting place of 11,953 Commonwealth casualties, including three winners of the Victoria Cross – two Australians (Captain C. S. Jeffries and Sergeant L. McGee) and a Canadian (Private James Robertson). Tyne Cot is an awesome reminder of the cost of war.

Our pilgrimage also included visits to the Messines Ridge, Hill 62, Hooge, Wytschaete, Bellewaerde Ridge and many other battlefields. Hooge, of course, straddling the Menin Road, was where Noel Chavasse won his Military Cross in June 1915, and where Billy Congreve VC, born on the Wirral, earned his Military Cross. Congreve and his father, Walter Norris Congreve, are one of only three father and son combinations to each win a VC, and both will feature in later volumes of this series. Many VCs were won in the Ypres Salient, including Chavasse's second VC. Thomas

Alfred 'Todger' Jones from Runcorn was wounded twice at Hill 60 before earning his VC on the Somme, and Thomas Mottershead VC, from Widnes, earned his VC when his plane was shot down over Ploegsteert Wood in 1917. (He is buried at Bailleul and we visited his grave to lay a wreath on behalf of members of his family.) William Ratcliffe VC MM (see Book 1) earned both of his medals at Messines, and Harold Ackroyd, born in Southport, earned his VC on the Menin Road before being killed in action ten days later at nearby Glencourse Wood. Ackroyd is buried at Birr Cross Roads Cemetery, where we laid a wreath in his memory. Eric Bent, John Molyneux (from St Helens), Eric Dougall, John O'Neill and Norman Harvey from Newton-le-Willows all won their VCs in this small area of Belgium. Donald Farmer, who is featured in this book and won his VC during the Boer War, was wounded here at Hooge.

Our visits also took in Sanctuary Wood Museum, the Canadian Memorial at Hill 62 and the Liverpool Scottish Memorial at Bellewaerde.

**Grave of Thomas Mottershead VC at Bailleul Military Cemetery**

Sombre and impressive as the cemeteries and war memorials are, in Ypres there should always be time to visit one of the many establishments – which Great War troops would have known as 'estaminets' - to raise a glass 'to absent friends' – all part of 'remembering'. The Old Bill bar resounded to the skirl of the pipes and the sound of the drums of the Clan Wallace Band!

Several of the VC winners I have mentioned feature in this book; others will be the subject of Books 3 and 4 in the future. The main purpose of our trip was to reinvigorate our enthusiasm for our project and to pay our respects to men whose deeds preserved for us so many of those freedoms which we so often take for granted. Its main effect was to make

**Grave of Harold Ackroyd VC at Birr Cross Roads Cemetery**

**Inscribed stone at the Liverpool Scottish Memorial at Bellewaerde**

us even more determined to rectify what seems to us to be a sad omission, and to honour these men as they deserve. You have helped us to do so by buying this book: we hope you have enjoyed it and would invite you to contact us if you wish to help our project in any way.

*Bill Sergeant and our Committee.*